Lean System Management for Leaders

A New Performance Management Toolset

Lean System Management for Leaders
A New Performance Management Toolset

By
Richard E. Mallory

Routledge
Taylor & Francis Group

A PRODUCTIVITY PRESS BOOK

Taylor & Francis
Boca Raton, London, New York

A Routledge title, part of the Taylor & Francis imprint, a member of the Taylor & Francis Group, the academic division of T&F Informa plc

Published in 2018 by Routledgea Taylor & Francis Group
711 Third Avenue, New York, NY 10017

No claim to original U.S. Government works
Printed in the United States of America on acid-free paper
10 9 8 7 6 5 4 3 2 1

International Standard Book Number-13: 978-1-138-48184-8 (Hardback)
International Standard Book Number-13: 978-1-351-05951-0 (eBook)

Visit the Taylor & Francis Web site at
http://www.taylorandfrancis.com

and the Productivity Press Web site at
http://www.productivitypress.com

Contents

About the Author

Richard E. Mallory has had a career focused on implementing quality science in the public sector. He is a certified project management professional (PMP) and has a Master of Arts in Management (MM). He has served for almost ten years as a senior executive in federal and state governments and as a consultant and trainer in quality practice for almost 20 years. He served as chair of the American Society for Quality Government Division in 2013–2014 and is currently a principal consultant for CPS HR Consulting in Sacramento, California. He is also the author of *Quality Standards for Highly Effective Government* (Second Edition, Taylor & Francis, 2018) and *Management Strategy: Creating Excellent Organizations* (Trafford Publishing, 2002). He is a seven-time examiner for the U.S. and California Baldrige Quality Awards and a career-long practitioner of quality in government.

He and his wife Cathy live in Orangevale, California, and have four grown children, Eric, Kevin, Joseph, and Julie.

He can be reached at rich_mallory@yahoo.com.

Introduction

When Dr. W. Edwards Deming wrote *Out of the Crisis* in 1982, he said that the aim of his book was the transformation of management, because traditional management had failed. His book is often recognized as the first clarion call for what is today regarded as *quality management*, outlining the practices and need for excellence in delivered products and services. Today, we might better describe his insight as the branch of management science focused on superior performance, and its goal as the sustained and predictable delivery of excellent products and services—the science of value creation. This book introduces the science of value creation with system science as its foundation. It both unifies and supplants the pre-existing notions of quality management.

It provides new analytic skills for leaders of all kinds to define a best known management, a best achievable practice, and an operational plan to accomplish superior results.

1

Introducing System Management

As with many disciplines, the concepts of quality management have been progressively interpreted and stylized by various practitioners over time, particularly through specific, successful applications of its use. Its predominant application today has been narrowed even more through the focused practice of Lean Six Sigma. Through that narrowing, it has largely failed and given up on the application of quality practice to entire organizational systems—even though they are essential to designing and sustaining quality practice over time.

This book will correct that problem and introduces a broad new framework for system management,* including practical tools and guidance for its use. It provides the long-promised "profound knowledge of systems" and shows how structured systems can unify and align quality practices throughout an entire organization. It also introduces a framework for objectively measuring the maturity of systems and processes† to provide an organizational quality scorecard, essential for sustainability.

Many research studies have shown that proven practices of performance excellence, or "quality," cannot be maintained over the long term. This book postulates that the reason for this failure is that there is no cohesive guidance on the management of groups of people working together toward specific goals.‡ Instead, we have only a patchwork application of two very

---

* The term *system management* will often be used in this book rather than its more common plural form, *systems management*, since the skills necessary for the management of a single system independently are required for precision of analysis and improvement. The management of a plurality of systems will be simple once the tools for system management are understood.
† Mallory, Richard, 2018. *Quality Standards for Highly Effective Government*. Second Edition, Taylor & Francis.
‡ Both the Baldrige Excellence Framework and ISO 9001 purport to provide such frameworks, but both their complexity and their lack of a system management standard have hobbled their broader use.

specific knowledge areas—one for process management and one for project management. That is the end of our management science as it applies to group practice, and we then try to patch it together with a generic body of knowledge which we call *leadership*. If individual leaders cannot pull it all together with vision, instinct, or charisma, some other books offer various "frameworks," which are sometimes described as *maps*. This is certainly not a body of science; it is akin to a box of puzzle pieces that we are trying to piece into a picture that no one can really describe!

Process management and project management are treated as distinct subcategories of all organizational management, so they cannot provide a structure for guiding the organization toward the use of fact-based management and structured problem solving everywhere. Much of the practice of leadership, then, is focused only on either one-to-one interactions with individuals—"supervision"—or generic group practices* such as "motivation," "goal-setting," or "encouraging the heart." The practice of "frameworks" is equally unscientific and provides a cook-book of advisory or prescriptive tactics under headings such as "Baldrige," "ISO," or "The House of Lean."

It is a great omission of current management knowledge that there is no framework for defining, analyzing, standardizing, or implementing continuous improvement in areas such as governance, strategic planning, budgeting, quality control, and program management.† These, and a number of other categories of organizational work, are defined as systems in this book, and are therefore opened to fact-based analysis and improvement through the described tools and practices it provides.

The use of scientific management on the noted systems is indeed possible, because systems are repetitive and cyclical and create definable outputs. For this reason, they offer an opportunity to learn and improve, and you will learn specific frameworks and tools for their definition and improvement.

Other repetitive, cyclical, and output-specific functions or systems include organizational goal-setting, decision-making, and oversight. Not only are these not viewed as subjects of fact-based analysis and improvement in the current management literature, but they are often viewed as either isolated activities or sequential decisions that are *only* manageable

---

* Generic group practices are not associated with a particular desired outcome or output and are believed to be associated with either a positive work environment or worker commitment to generalized goals.

† Appendix III presents the Roles of Management as systems.

through spontaneous or consultative decision-making by individual managers. Similar attitudes also exist regarding the management of a program, or a program office, and all of this structuring and decision-making is therefore incorrectly left to the judgment of a single executive.

This kind of thinking—which could be called *leadership despotism*—leads to the conclusion that the actions of executives are somehow above or isolated from the application of Lean and quality science. This in turn leads these managers to believe that the actions, events, and activities they use for decision-making and program direction should not and cannot be standardized and documented. They incorrectly believe that executive actions should be created by their individual intuition and contemporaneous judgments, which also means that they are reactive and insulated from organizational wisdom. This belief must change!

System management and systems science,* introduced for the first time in this book, references the fact that any management outcome created through repetitive and predictable components is ideally suited to fact-based management, to the application of the well-known principles of quality science, and to participation by empowered and engaged employees. This opens the door to structured learning and improvement throughout the organization, as well as achievement of superior results. This indeed is the learning organization envisioned by Peter Senge in his famous work *The Fifth Discipline*.

This book therefore opens a broad new horizon for management science and a new foundation for understanding and improving organizations. It presents a structured framework for defining and controlling organizations, along with a system maturity standard that allows regular measurement of the maturity and capability of defined management systems. In this way, it provides an agile framework for the organization-wide practice of quality (which we will refer to as *performance excellence*†) and

---

* The terms *quality science* and *process science* refer to the tools and knowledge associated with quality management. These had their origins in the Toyota Production System of the 1970s, embrace a broad body of professional knowledge focused on doing work right the first time, and are embodied in the Body of Knowledge maintained by the American Society for Quality. The terms *system management* and *system science* are described in this book and very broadly defined in the Baldrige Excellence Framework of the National Institute of Standards and Technology (NIST) Baldrige Performance Excellence Program. It is a new practice that will redefine the framework of quality.

† *Performance excellence* should be the preferred term to *quality* in the 21st century, in that it captures the essence of what the quality industry attempts to achieve. Its practice is then focused on all systems and processes that create value and not just the end product or service that results from this activity.

enables the use of a system maturity scorecard showing the capability and maturity of quality management function throughout the organization. It also allows and enables an organization-wide scorecard on the practice of quality at the process level through use of the process management standard.* The combination of system management with process management enables the consistent and sustainable use of quality practice and corrects the single major failure of quality practices everywhere. The alignment of structured system and process management practices creates an agile and continuing quality framework throughout the organization.

This book refers to system management in the singular for two reasons. First, there is a need to distinguish system management from the generic term *systems management* that fills conceptual management theory. Second, this book introduces a form of system management that is so specific and tactical that it must be a measured requirement of all future management. It is not a theory but a daily management practice.

It also reconciles the differences between project management and process management, in that system management also creates a comprehensive framework for projects that is consistent with the process management body of knowledge. Lastly, it solves the problems of application of process management to unique and tailored deliverables, which are created by variable work groups.

The structured system management framework provided in this book provides specific rules and tools for identifying and modeling key organizational systems (each one in the singular) and for their alignment in a system of Lean, quality, and continuous improvement. Its maturity standards allow measurement of the depth and completeness of the adoption of quality practices in each key system and process and overall in the business unit and the organization.

This is designed as a workbook, and is presented sequentially, so that you can immediately test its theory and value as you use it. Because it is a workbook, it will provide necessary background theory in the Appendices.† This allows you, the reader, to quickly understand these new tools, to apply them to your specific circumstances, and to rapidly devise implementation plans.

---

* See Mallory, Richard, September 2016. "Measuring Maturity, Quality Progress." http://asq.org/quality-progress/2016/09/process-capability/measuring-maturity.html.

† Two white papers on the theory and practice of system management are provided in Appendices III and IV.

This overall presentation then allows Chapter 2 to begin with the necessary descriptions and definitions of processes, systems, and projects; the chapter wraps up with a description of how systems management combines with process management to provide an overall organization-wide framework for management and change. Chapters 3–6 then present the tools and practices necessary for the identification and control of your systems through system mapping.

Chapter 7 introduces the use of the system management standard to objectively score process maturity, while Chapters 8–10 show how system management fits together with process management and project management to create an agile framework for organizational quality.

The use of structured system mapping and maturity scoring is a pioneering discipline in management science, which can forever change its practice. It opens the door to a profound new understanding of structured and designed systems with the potential to create another giant leap forward in the efficiency, effectiveness, and delivered value of all managed work enterprises.

2

Systems, Processes, and Projects—And Their Role in Managing Work

There are only four basic kinds of work in organizations. There are activities, processes, projects, and systems. Activities are *one-offs*, or *things that are done for which there is very little precedent and that will only be done one time.* So for example, if auditors show up in your office and a superior asks for someone to get them lunch, one or more people will have to invent a good way to do the job. However they do it will never be written down, will never be repeated, and will soon be forgotten. This is a classic activity, in that its work method is spontaneous and invented. It is guided by few rules,* there will be no repetition, and there is no need to learn and improve.

Process is probably the most familiar and over-used term in management, and is generally defined as *a set of defined incremental activities that transform an input to a valuable output for an end-user or customer.* The term *process* as discussed in this workbook will typically refer to high-volume workflow that is completed by a formally structured group of persons, each doing specialized tasks. The output of a process is generally standardized and uniform, so that any variation in the output is not typical. The "science" of standardizing and controlling process began in 1923 with the presentation of a professional paper on process flowcharting by Frank B. Gilbreth Sr., and then continued with many books on Lean and continuous quality improvement throughout the 1900s.†

---

* Organizational policy or ethical standards may impose a few rules. In this case, it is likely that policy will prohibit the consumption of alcoholic beverages in government offices, and ethical rules may require auditors to pay the cost of their own lunch.
† A bibliography of the author's favorite books on Lean and process improvement is provided in Appendix IV.

Project is probably the second most familiar term in management and is *a temporary endeavor undertaken to create a unique product, service, or result of lasting benefit. It generally has a fixed resource base and a project team that will disband on project completion.* While any specific project is done just once, the project team members and their organization will often work on many projects over the course of many years, and so, their knowledge and practice are repeated. In this manner, while projects are often thought to be "unique," there is great value found in performing "lessons learned" reviews after each effort to learn and understand from the cyclic features of projects collectively. This is one of the underlying principles of system management and the reason why it holds great promise for project management. As a result, we will treat projects as a subcategory of systems.

System is the least understood management term, and when used, it generally implies a repetitive group of practices. Our definition will be *a well-ordered and repeatable approach to completing required and specific work outputs.* The primary distinguishing feature of a human system is that it is comprised of an intent to do something, initiated by leadership or intent (or "logos"); that it seeks to control resources; and that it has a specific "aim" or purpose. It is for this reason that the purpose of your system will be the first topic covered in the next chapter.

This book deals with human systems and their intent through leadership to achieve outcomes (an influence on the larger organization or world) through the creation of products, services, plans, mental models, and other kinds of specific "outputs."

In this work, management systems are considered to be the repetitive and important workflows of executive and program management offices or of project management—any of which *should* have a well-defined purpose and method, but probably often do not. Defined systems may include a rather broad focus, as in organizational governance, organizational oversight, and quality management systems; *or,* they may include rather specific executive management functions, such as the annual budget process, hiring and recruitment, or management of the safety program. In any case, we will regard management systems as a deliberate construction of management* and the only one that can link processes end-to-end to each other and to reporting systems, strategy, controls, authority, support, and resources. So while the skeptical reader may want to dismiss

---

* As with processes, management systems may be poorly designed and operated in their "native" state but will be refined and continuously improved through the application of systems management.

the concept of system as being adequately defined at present, because it is so fundamental and ubiquitous, this book will focus on a clearer and more objective definition. This workbook will rely on the demonstration of valuable tools for management and improvement of systems as a currently unmet need of management science.*

The profound knowledge inherent in this analytic structure is that almost all of the work of every organization can be defined through its use, and, therefore, a structured quality/performance framework can be developed. Through an understanding and simple application of all of these frameworks, the practice of management will be transformed.

However, to use these three frameworks, you will need to know how they are the same and how they are different, which is what we will cover next in this chapter. We will also want to know how systems management combines with process management to provide an overall organization-wide framework for management and change, and that will be covered in Chapters 8 and 9.

PROCESSES, PROJECTS, AND SYSTEMS—WHAT IS DIFFERENT AND WHAT IS THE SAME?

Looking again at the four categories of work initially described above, we can see that activities are the only type of work done just once and forgotten, while the other three categories (process, project, and system) are performed on a *repetitive* basis. And even though each project is defined as a one-time activity, a series of projects will be performed by any work group or organization over a period of time. So while a single project may be unique, project management is cyclical and can therefore benefit from lessons learned. The knowledge base of the organization regarding projects can grow and improve.

It is therefore apparent that *most* of the important work of our organizations and *most* of their high-value work is repetitive in this manner. This observation frames our first conclusion: that the active management of processes, projects, and systems is our highest-value work, and that it is all repetitive.

---

* See Appendix III for further background on systems theory in the white paper entitled "Systems Management to Launch the Next Era of Quality."

The fact that it is repetitive means that we can observe its cycles and learn from that experience. In many ways, our repetitive work will have a predictable pattern of practice, so that we can learn and improve its outcome in the future. Just as we do in project management, we can always conduct lessons learned and look for repetitive patterns of best practice.*

The shared characteristic of all repetitive work is a *defined purpose or outcome*, achieved through the creation of specific work outputs, and through which we evaluate or measure its success. In fact, this is one of the major differences between what we might call *traditional management*, the kind that Dr. Deming said "had failed," and the management of quality science, which has periodically created the highest levels of innovation, productivity, and performance ever seen. The primary significant difference is in the act of defining requirements for its output so that operational efficiency can be measured, as shown in Figure 2.1.

In process, we say that the requirements of the process are determined by the customer,† and we can turn to the customer as the basis of measurement. Regardless, the definition of a preferred best outcome to each process, project, and system is possible, and the establishment of precise and measurable criteria of success is the first factor for optimal performance (or "quality") management.

FIGURE 2.1
Showing how a measured, objective standard differentiates traditional management from quality management.

---

* In some cases, these lessons learned are contained in professional literature as *best practices* or as work guides. All of professional knowledge, of medicine for example, will define the best practices of its systematic application.

† An exclusive focus on a customer is not sufficient in all instances, and certainly not for regulatory, evaluative (as in insurance claims), audit, or caretaker processes. The establishment of criteria for most successful outcomes is still possible, however, leading to the term *process design requirements* used in this book. A single process customer can best be understood as a process stakeholder.

All three types of repetitive work can be more fully explained by the unifying theory of work management, which is new to quality science, and which seeks to identify the delivery components of repetitive work. In this way, it provides the points of control through which we can make it more predictable and manageable. It will also create the basis for managers to learn from past experience and constructively apply that learning to the future so that better results, or improvement, can take place.* It is presented in Figure 2.2.

In Figure 2.2, the factors of possible commonality are categorized as the uniformity of the production environment and the uniformity of the people, steps, and methods within that environment.† It is acknowledged that these categories are not entirely distinct and mutually exclusive in their definition, and that the combination of factors is somewhat arbitrary. So in fact, the factors involved in the uniformity of the people—presumably skills, training, job definition, and task definition—are separated from the uniformity of steps and methods.

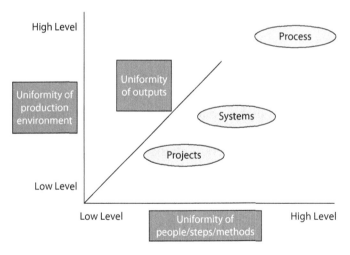

FIGURE 2.2
Unifying theory of work management.

---

* It is the author's belief that this is what Dr. Deming was referencing in his "theory of knowledge" as one part of the system of profound knowledge: specifically, that all process control and systems control is an expression of human learning and continuous improvement.

† This line of thought regarding the methods of standardized work was also noted in *The Structuring of Organizations*, by Henry Mintzberg, 1979, pp. 3–9.

That said, however, let us begin with the uniformity of the people who create the work output, whether through process, project, or system, *because* our management actions to standardize key performance attributes in each group will help us to predictably and consistently deliver excellent output. Following this line of thought, we can see how many traditional management practices should help us in this regard.

Specifically, we see that hiring employees with specific baseline knowledge, skills, and abilities is one way to create uniformity of people, and that the principle of uniformity does not mean that all are the same but that each group, and successors in those positions, meet a uniform minimum standard for that job. The repetitive series of actions to identify those skills, and to hire and place employees who match those skills, is both a system and a key practice for the integrity of all other processes, projects, and systems throughout the organization. This observation points to the thesis of this book, that through defining systems and processes, and aligning those systems and processes, we will have developed a perfect agile framework for performance excellence, or quality.

Similarly, the training of employees to meet those requirements is another important underlying factor, and the repetitive series of actions that creates that training is another organization-wide system.*

Finally—especially with systems and projects—getting people to buy in to a sense of responsibility for fully and completely fulfilling the correct actions necessary to obtain the highest-value output is critical to the achievement of that highest-value output. The observation that there is a need for a uniformity of methods, steps, or both to achieve the highest levels of output in repetitive work supports the idea that there is a preferred and learned *best known practice*, which is another foundation of excellent work.

In this notation of a best known practice, we can also see that processes are specific enough that we can expect to map one very specific path through the series of work tasks that exist between input and output and that we can expect to be able to assign very specific tasks to each person assigned a part of this work. Indeed, those who carry out the work process generally have specific job assignments that are embedded in these associated work processes.

Systems and projects, on the other hand, are often completed through a series of *activity groups* or milestones that exist between the input and

---

* The structuring of this system will be an example in Chapter 5.

the output. There is no one specific and sequential path, and there is not a dedicated team to carry out the work. This does not mean, however, that there is not a set of best known practices, as is demonstrated by the project management body of knowledge (PMBOK)* and the project management practices of every project management office. The same is true of systems, and even though executive management often fail to either identify or document best management practices for systems, this does not mean that they do not exist.

So, for example, while it is generally known in most organizations that the system of budgeting should begin with requests from operating divisions that are based on an assessment of current operational performance and future needs, that is not always done. And while getting a two-way discussion between operational executives and financial executives regarding goals and priorities for budgeting is also a best practice, that does not always occur either. A busy and chaotic world (and sometimes, a political world) will often short-cut and abridge best known practice. Likewise, in the area of project management, the development of a project plan and schedule, with a regularly recurring update of results against that plan, is a best known practice. However, we also know that those practices, too, are often short-cut and abridged.†

The level of development and documentation‡ of a best known practice then becomes another factor in the maturity and capability of a process, project, or system. It is certainly far easier to use a best known practice when it has been prepared and is "on the shelf." Where it has not even been developed, it may exist only in the individual knowledge of some of those who must carry it out, and their knowledge of what to do may also be fragmentary. Likewise, where the best known practice is available and expected, it is far easier to make assignments or (in the case of systems and projects) to negotiate responsibilities. It is far easier to mobilize a team and establish skills when at least the activity groups and milestones are defined.

---

* Many practitioners feel that while PMBOK provides situational guidance, there is not just one path to follow.

† It is acknowledged that one impediment to a single rigid structure is the perception by some that it will inhibit innovation. It should be understood that there is a difference between technical innovation and structuring processes after a single best known practice has been established. Also, the organizational culture should continue to allow and encourage the examination of best known practice and the adoption of future improvements.

‡ Process documentation can take several forms but often includes a process flowchart, supporting procedures, templates, desk manuals, standards, and similar work aids.

This raises the issue of what we might call *native* systems, which operate on their own volition, versus what we might call *structured* or *managed* systems, which have been identified by executive leadership as critical to operational success. Structured systems demand a disciplined and structured approach as the basis of improved operations. Organizations as well as societies do many things through "common knowledge," habit, and culture, and while these sometimes turn out well, they can often turn out badly. Simple things are mostly likely to do well in a native condition. In one of the best known examples, Americans are almost always open to the idea of standing in line and taking turns. These are examples of *native systems*, which exist without any imposed design or structure. Our free market economy is another native system, and government efforts to influence its result become an engineered system imposed on a native system. So, the interplay of systems is also an important management concept, which is touched on in later chapters.

One definition of politics in organizations is how things get done when there are no rules, order, and instructions. When that is the case, either workers improvise or leaders make decisions and give incremental task orders based on political agendas or individual judgments without regard to analysis or past learning experience. Failed projects often operate without systematic structure and without regard to best known practice. Likewise, the operation of a system of training will often not go well or have good results as a native system. So, we can see the importance of the imposition of an appropriate level of best practice steps and methods.

This raises a more interesting observation regarding systems. The existence of a system as a structured or managed system depends on a collective shared knowledge, necessary to define its purpose, its best known practices, and its subordinate activity groups. This kind of disciplined and structured look is often the result of leadership interest* in developing this "logical path" for the work to follow.

The factors of uniformity of the production environment are obviously more applicable to processes than to projects and systems, since processes are often completed by a dedicated work team in a controlled and dedicated physical facility. In such an environment, the reliability and alignment of computer systems, office machines, and production facilities can be much more closely controlled. Those who are familiar with Lean

---

* Informal leadership and other types of interest may also be sufficient to motivate a logical ordering—or logos—that drives system management and improvement.

process methods may immediately recognize that the use of visual management techniques and an emphasis on Five "S" methodologies* are both much easier in such a controlled physical environment.

Projects and systems, on the other hand, may need to operate in many and various environments, and their designated leaders may even depend on things (subcontractors or computer systems) over which they have NO control. One of the most distinguishing factors between systems and processes is the need to plan for intervening variables and risks over which there is little or no control.

Similarly, the control of inputs into such repetitive cyclical workflows, sometimes called *supply management,* is likely to be much more controllable for processes than it is for projects and systems, even though the *attempt* to control such inputs is equally important to all.

Finally, we can see that the specific characteristics of the product or service created by a project or system are much more likely to be different from cycle to cycle than they will be for a process. Indeed, the specialization of work production in processes is one of the things that enable the specialization of assigned labor and the specificity of the tasks necessary to create it. This does not mean that it is not important to precisely specify the output requirements of systems and processes—only that it is likely that the value creation process will need to be adaptable to respond to unforeseen changes during each cycle of its operation.

We will use our awareness of how they are the same and how they are different so that we can best identify the measurable attributes and management framework most appropriate to manage each, and their level of compliance (native versus engineered/managed) to determine the maturity of the process or system.[†] Table 2.1 will provide a quick reference guide.

So as you think about the structured work created by your organization, if it is repetitive and cyclical, you can presume that either a process model or a system model should be used to ensure management best practices, even if we are looking at work done by front line service providers. You will find that a great deal of the work of all organizations is best structured and managed using a system focus.

---

* Sort, straighten, shine, set in order, and standardize.
[†] We will allow project management to fall into the background at this point and will use the term *system management* as the ordinate principle.

TABLE 2.1

Characteristics of Process, Project, and System—Similarities and Differences

	Process	Project	System
Defined desired outcome—purpose or "aim"	Yes. The outputs of each process cycle are always very similar, if not identical, and the measurable attributes of the deliverable are also highly uniform	Yes, although even within specific projects, changes and adaptations are expected. This could include changes in the number of deliverables (as in agile) or in the configuration or characteristics of each deliverable	Yes. While the purpose or function of each system is clear and unchanging, the steps, methods, and characteristics of the delivered product or service may have a high degree of variance. A system of "emergency response," for example, may have great variance in the services provided
Observable cycles	Yes—sometimes process cycles are in minutes, sometimes in days	Yes, although single project cycles may be from one month to years long. The project management practices in an organization are a form of system, and only the events of evaluating and improving those methods are cyclical, on a varying schedule	Mostly. Executive and program systems usually support operations and process, so they are typically annual. Some systems (such as marketing) may not have any single, specific deliverable, and so, only their evaluation and improvement events would be cyclical
Single best path— same steps in same order	Yes. Process management strives to standardize the steps and order to obtain best results	No. Projects must respond to frequent variation in conditions and personnel and perform tasks in parallel, when possible, or in sequence, when required	No. Systems must also respond to variation in conditions and personnel. Some outputs are produced in a network configuration.* No single path exists
Single dedicated team	Yes. Projects often can count on a dedicated workforce performing the work, and often, their job requirements are directly aligned with process requirements	No. Project teams are often made up of people whose project tasks are only a small part or no part of their current job requirements	Partially. While systems are sometimes made up of personnel whose job is directly linked to the system's performance, the contribution of many others—inside and outside the organization—may be required

(Continued)

TABLE 2.1 (CONTINUED)

Characteristics of Process, Project, and System—Similarities and Differences

	Process	Project	System
Best known practice	Yes. Excellent projects seek to maintain a high level of specificity in tasks, task requirements, and sequence (or flow)	Yes, but only in activity groups, in project management oversight, and in the achievement of defined requirements for milestones	Yes. As with projects, best practices apply within activity groups, in the oversight of each cycle, and in the achievement of defined requirements for milestones
Formal decision points	Yes. Processes must have rigid go/no-go decision points necessary to ensure quality in the delivered product/service	No. While some project criteria may have rigid and inflexible acceptance criteria, a range of acceptability exists at many other points	No. Many systems allow intrinsic quality criteria to be flexible to allow for changes in the delivered product/service, the effort required to deliver it, or the timing of delivery
Output requirements—variance in attributes of what is produced	No	Somewhat. Projects will generally have output requirements on delivered portions of work and outcome statements for the project as a whole. There may be negation of delivered segments and output requirements to achieve the bigger (or primary) purpose and to keep within budget and schedule	Yes. Systems have a defined purpose (outcome) but can significantly modify the steps and actions used and, hence, the quality of the end deliverable. The output of systems is often highly variable
Expectation that the defined cycle will be interrupted	No. Lean calls for continuous flow, and it is a primary goal of process management to avoid stoppage and interruption	No. Projects also emphasize continuous delivery and track the critical path to avoid stoppage and interruption	Yes. Systems must anticipate intervening variables and have a plan to accommodate them. That is one of the defining attributes of a system

* See Figure 8.3 for discussion of the network configuration.

For example, if we look at healthcare services provided to patients in a hospital, we can see that there are standardized positions (nurses) visiting patient bedsides, doing a variety of diagnostics, and providing a variety of types of services as needed. The lack of a uniform set of tasks—a defined single path—and the diversity of types of responses—that is, highly variable output requirements that might be needed—should be tip-offs that this is NOT a process. If we were looking at the dispensing of patient medications, we would see a single path of steps and tasks that should occur in a particular order and that result in a uniform outcome. THIS would be best managed with a process model.

Likewise, if you were to review the work stream associated with an in-house counsel rendering a legal opinion, you would again see a variety of activities performed, based on the specific aspects of the matter under review and resulting in an opinion spanning various subjects with various levels of certainty. This work is best managed as a system. However, if legal office review of contracts is involved, it is much more likely that a process model will suffice.

In the previous two examples, there was a generalized component of work that could be subdivided into process work, but this is not always true. The annual evaluation and prioritization of routine maintenance needs in a sewer collection system may only be systematic. We know that it is systematic, because the outcome can be defined, even though the specific tasks and actions selected (the number and nature of service actions chosen) are negotiable. Even though the selection of such work may be driven by policy or service protocols that make it more process oriented, the likelihood of significant intervening variables makes system management techniques more applicable.

The power of system management to bring order and analytic method to *most* of the structured work output of organizations, and to make it subject to fact-based management to continuous improvement methodologies, is profound. The next chapter will present mapping and analysis tools that are new to management and that provide a lean and agile framework for organizational transformation.

As you review the structured work activities in your organization, Table 2.1 will help you to distinguish the differences and to then pick the best tool for its best practice operation and for its improvement. A clear recognition of the two forms is important to proceed. It is important to be able to understand what constitutes a system and what constitutes a process, so that you use appropriate diagnostic and improvement techniques as part of your management practice.

3

Starting Your System Map

System mapping is a tool that is used to define and document *best known management practices* and then to establish a *best achievable practice* that reflects your ability to deliver on that best practice. System mapping supports analytic and design steps to create a structured/designed system, operating in a native system environment, to facilitate a consistent, predictable result.* The best possible practice for your structured/designed system may be tempered by your available resources, work environment, and priorities. Once that best possible practice is standardized and documented, it will provide a template and guide for you in the achievement of superior business results.

The steps in system mapping will be described further in this chapter, and in succeeding chapters, and are identified here simply to provide you with a map of what is to follow. Do not get discouraged if you do not understand what is expected in each step. The steps are:

1. Identify and name the system from which you are seeking optimized outputs.
2. Identify its outputs and business purpose (or "aim").
3. Identify the principal activity groups associated with its intended value creation.
4. Identify the output criteria of each principal activity group.
5. Identify the influencing factors that are causes of successful outputs.
6. Describe the attributes of successful performance of each principal activity group.

---

* *Native systems* are those that currently exist in an open environment, often only informally structured. The purpose of this book is to show leadership how to use engineered systems to improve current results. Later chapters will talk about *intervening variables*, which are often unplanned or unpredictable inputs into our structured and designed system, often from a native system.

7. Describe the indicators and measures of success for the activity groups.
8. Describe the indicators and measures of failure for the activity groups.
9. Identify the most feasible points of control for your system (the best achievable practice—and a system operational plan).
10. Identify intervening variables within your system.
11. Develop a risk management plan and risk management scenarios.
12. Apply the system management standard to understand your system capacity and system maturity and the next steps for systems control and improvement efforts.

In process science, the Define, Measure, Analyze, Improve, and Control (DMAIC) improvement model* is widely recognized, and that same map can be used in system science.† However, it is not well recognized that the first use, or cycle, of the DMAIC model is used to understand and to standardize processes and systems, and it will also be used for that purpose in system mapping and control. The wisdom of the saying that "you have to walk before you can run" is widely recognized, and in both process science and system science, you have to standardize a best achievable practice before you can improve it.

The first phase of our efforts is the design and documentation of a best possible system management practice, which we will call a *best known practice*.‡ The second phase is to deploy and standardize its use, which we will call a *best achievable practice*. The third phase is to monitor and analyze its performance. The fourth phase provides the basis for continuous improvement. Capably moving from the first phase to the fourth phase may take one or more system cycles and is shown in Figure 3.1.

Our beginning point is for you to select a key system for mapping, to create an "engineered" design that will provide the hoped-for results, to standardize the management approach and deployment that will create that result, and then, to progressively improve it over time.

---

* A diagram showing how DMAIC is intended to be used is provided in Chapter 7.
† Process managers can also use this systems management methodology to augment traditional process management tools, and to apply it more effectively using a system management approach. This is presented in Chapter 8.
‡ We can assume that each phase may include a review and update of the 12 steps noted earlier, although with a much greater understanding and awareness in each repetition.

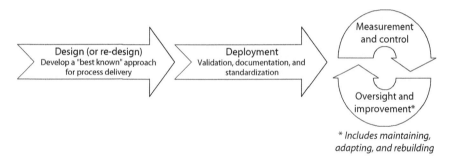

FIGURE 3.1
Four phases of process and system management.

The key system you select should be an area of opportunity for you, depending either on its importance to your overall job or program objectives, or on a deficiency that may now exist in its performance.

System mapping can be first done at a high level—for example, at a level reflecting all the work of a single program office—and then later focused into component parts. Likewise, executive managers can select very high-level outcomes for system mapping and can profitably map areas such as organizational oversight, safety management, or capital planning. However, it is important to remember that system maps, like process maps, are a management tool, and our effort to document them is a reflection of our desire to improve that workflow. Your focused thought and attention will be required to obtain any benefit, so the selection of areas of marginal interest will not create the level of interest necessary to carry you through to completion.

Once you recognize the power of systems mapping, you may have a desire to "map everything," but you will still get best results if you can focus initially on areas of greatest importance and need.

The need to focus is also based on the fact that time for improvement could reduce your time for running your current operations. No matter how beneficial or interesting this may be, you will need to prioritize. Generally speaking, your highest-priority system should be the one that your customers and external stakeholders feel is *what you do* and reflects a primary and important purpose. This selected system may also define the work in your span of control that has influence over

- The greatest number of actions or people
- The biggest part of your time
- The largest impact on your program success

If the management focus or program objective of your unit offers several possible systems of importance, you may wish to give first attention to the one that has the greatest performance "gap" or that is creating greatest concern. Keep in mind that you can system map an entire program office or unit using only its title, even though a more refined focus on a specific outcome of that office may be better.* If you are mapping an executive function such as "budget oversight," that generalized title will work. Whatever your goal, that should be your identified key system in mind, and with that description in mind, you are now ready to begin.

DEFINE SYSTEM PURPOSE

Three short exercises (or "steps") will get you started:

1. *List the outputs of your identified system*: Create a list of the specific things that are produced by your defined system. Develop a list of the specific outputs of your office—the things that you hand off or deliver to a next user.† It is often helpful to remember that these things should be described in specific enough terms that you could see them or count them. This can be a long, bulleted list of outputs.

2. *Describe the business purpose‡ of your program or unit*: Create a series of short statements that describe the business purpose of your system and that could best explain to an outsider what the value add of your system really is. These statements should encapsulate what it does (and for whom) that creates business value. (Hint: You don't need to list the "who," but do keep in mind that the determination of "value add" is by linking "what" you do to a specific user.)

---

* You may therefore insert the term *business unit* or *program office* to replace the word "system" in the succeeding text. As you will see through use, both business units and program offices are encompassed by systems management. System maps can also be refined through the analysis of "sub-systems" if desired.

† The terms *outputs* and *outcomes* are often confused. *Output* refers to specific describable (and usually countable) things that are produced and delivered to others at the end of a work cycle of a system or business unit. *Outcomes* are a secondary consequence of the outputs, even if they are the intended ultimate result of the work. So, the government office that issues fishing licenses has an output of licenses but an expected outcome of a healthier fishery. Outcomes are also often expressed in the business purpose of the unit or system.

‡ Other possible terms for *business purpose* are *aim* or *objective*. As noted earlier, the business purpose often mirrors the intended outcomes of the unit. Business purpose for a government or a nonprofit is a description of the value it brings to the greater world.

3. *Name the system you will map:* This could include elements such as the name of the program unit in which you work, *or* the *purpose* of the work effort as created in Step 2.*

If we were to use human resources division operations as our system mapping focus, we might decide that its outputs included such things as

- Recruitment events
- Hiring lists
- Selection panels
- Appointments
- Orientations
- Training activities
- Issuance of pay
- Benefit enrollments and change
- Adverse actions
- Process retirements

We could also list the *outcomes* of these activities to include the purpose of doing these things. If we did so, the outcomes might include some of the following:

- An efficient and effective workforce in all programs
- Happy and motivated employees, who are able to find career advancement
- A timely, positive response to the needs of employees and supervisors
- A safe and positive work environment

The development of both outputs and outcomes will lead us to a description of business purpose: in this case, finding, recruiting, placing, and training excellent employees throughout the organization to ensure that all allocated vacant positions are promptly filled. There is an obvious parallel between the outcome statement and business purpose, which makes business purpose easy to define.

This is all important pre-work before our next step of defining the primary activity groups of our system.

---

* System mapping can also be used to engineer a system in the larger world, such as "controlling voter fraud," so the nature of the result desired may also be an appropriate name.

However, before we proceed, there is one more check that will be helpful, and that will be to review the goals established for you or your business unit and the connection between your system and the strategic plan of the organization. In making that connection, you may find a need to more closely align your system or its priority outcomes to the organization-wide plan, and this alignment with other systems in the organization will be very helpful in assuring your best results.*

If we had identified our organizational Human Resources Division as the subject of mapping, we could say that the business purpose is:

- To recruit, hire, train, and maintain a capable and motivated workforce. To develop and maintain a positive and productive workplace.

While there is no one correct way to complete these first three exercises, the development of a matrix might help. It is also suggested that because of the tactical way that most workers and managers think about work, the easiest first step is to brainstorm the list of outputs—the specific things produced (or that you would like produced). So, in the human resources division example, we could create a matrix as in Table 3.1.

Given all of that, we still may want to simply name our system map "Human Resources Program" or something more specific, such as "Providing a Capable and Motivated Workforce." Either would work.

You will see, of course, that the five columns shown again reflect the action steps for the creation of our overall system map, and we are now doing just the first and the last steps. Outcomes reflect the impacts of your system on the larger world, rather than just the specific things you produce, and are also indicative of the business purpose and mission. In this sense, the development of each column will refine and define the others. This overall effort must use descriptive and subjective terms and will therefore be subject to some interpretation and creative effort. The terms you use are foundational, though, so be sure they reflect reality and good business sense. When you are done, you can begin your system map using the format shown in Figure 3.2.

---

* Later on, we will also want to align your system with key processes to which it may supply inputs or from which it may receive outputs.

TABLE 3.1

Initial Documentation: Human Resources System

System Name				
Business Purpose/ Mission	**Principal Activity Groups/ Milestones**	**Influencing Factors**	**Outputs:**	**Outcomes:**
To recruit, hire, train, and maintain a capable and motivated workforce. To develop and maintain a positive and productive workplace.			• Recruiting events • Vacancy notices • Job descriptions • Interview panels • Hiring actions • Onboarding • Individual development plans • Training needs assessment • Training monitoring • Employee benefit actions • Employee satisfaction surveys	• An efficient and effective workforce in all programs • Happy and motivated employees who are able to find career advancement • A safe and positive work environment

FIGURE 3.2
First simple template for creation of a system map.

This initial analysis is critical to a more detailed system mapping and, specifically, to defining the *primary activity groups* and *milestones* that are the elements of our system map. Those, in turn, will be foundational to the creation of the *influencing factors* of system success that represent the second level of our map. These are covered in the next chapter.

4

Defining Principal Activity Groups

The next step in creating a map of a structured and defined system is to define the principal activity groups associated with your system. Figure 4.1 shows an example of such principal activity groups reflecting the human resources division example in the previous chapter.

The "base plate" symbol used to represent primary activity groups in the system map was selected both to distinguish it from the "tasks" of a process map and to represent that each activity group provides necessary building blocks for best-quality system outputs. The primary activity groups listed do not have to be sequential and are not a specific path to follow as in a process flow chart. Each principal activity group should represent a coherent grouping of tasks necessary to achieve a defined value add specific to that activity group. And while the group of tasks and activities that are followed to create the output of a principal activity group may vary, the attributes of its successful completion should be specific and measurable. There should be a requirements statement associated with each one. Principal activity groups can also be looked at as "business platforms" and may represent a practiced professional competency necessary for business success. Even so, the attributes for successful completion of each "cycle" of a principal activity group must be specific and measurable, as we will further discuss in Chapter 6.

The set of principal activity groups included in your system map should reflect all the value added actions necessary to complete your system

FIGURE 4.1
Providing a capable and motivated workforce.

objective and business purpose. Your principal activity groups should define and create the outline for the best management practices of the operation of this system.* Also, do not be surprised to find that each principal activity group may include a key process.

Your efforts to create a system map should lead you to design a "best known management practice" and then a "best achievable practice," which by itself is likely to improve its performance and your results. Similarly, its standardization and definition of requirements will enable your efforts to gather relevant data, study its results, and initiate continuous improvement.

As with any new idea, some may want to challenge the value of doing such a system map, but there are many benefits. These include: (1) providing a tool for the analysis and definition of best management practices; (2) assisting with system design and approach; (3) providing a basis for the specialization of work group teams or jobs within a larger unit; and (4) a work breakdown structure in projects.

Because we are trying to create an engineered system to provide value from a native system, such as a poorly ordered human organization or a poorly ordered group of organizations, these activity groups may not exist today[†] and will reflect the value chain to best create the outputs and outcomes desired. We can also refer to primary activity groups as project milestones or project phases.[‡] Primary activity groups are coherent groups of tasks required to create the specific value added outputs that are desired.

---

* Similarly to the baseball "home base" symbol, we could think of each principal activity group as being made up of a group of activities that are carried out at "first base," "second base," and so on.
[†] See Appendix IV for further information on native and engineered systems. For those working within a single organizational context, most of the system components may be controllable, while those who are using systems management to influence outcomes in the general population (for example, reducing recidivism of released prisoners) may find that many factors can only be influenced or responded to, rather than controlled.
[‡] The use of terms from the project management body of knowledge (PMBOK) is deliberate, as system mapping is in fact an effective framework for project management, and their use will provide a way to define best practices in project delivery. The design of primary activity groups should align around specific value added outputs in the same manner as project phases.

REFINING AND FINALIZING THE SELECTION
OF PRINCIPAL ACTIVITY GROUPS

The selection of principal activity groups is not an exact science, especially at first, and will be tested in several ways as you move forward. The first way is through the development of matching *outcome attributes*. So, after the group is named, ask:

- What would be the attributes or descriptive characteristics of complete success in this activity group?
- Or, alternately, what would be the attributes or characteristics of complete failure in this activity group?

It is likely you will find that expressions of "failure" or negative results in each activity group easily pair with expressions of successful outputs and are opposite.* So, in other words, the expression of "inability to fill positions" will be the opposite of "all positions quickly filled with qualified candidates." The two tests will work together to define the output requirements of each activity group.

So, for example, if you were using the "Satisfaction/ Retention" principal activity group in this example, you might first list negative results—or what the results of a "failure" to achieve the intended goal would be. This might produce a list like the following:

- Unmotivated and unproductive employees
- Personnel problems
- High leave use
- Employees leaving for other jobs in their first year

Then, turning to the descriptive characteristics of complete success in this activity group may now be a lot easier, and our list could include:

- Employees achieving praise and recognition
- High supervisor rankings at end of probationary period
- Employees completing additional job training

---

* It is the author's observation that it is often easier for individuals and groups to define negative outcomes rather than positive outcomes, even though the two are often different reflections of the same attribute.

- Job classification step increases based on merit
- New hires still working for the company after two years

Any of these attributes could then be built into a metric or an indicator to reflect the success of the principal activity group, and some will also apply to the positive functioning of the entire defined system. Following this through for all activity groups in your system will produce a model like that shown in Figure 4.2.

Looking at the "Hiring and Recruiting" activity group, we might then say that our metrics and indicators would include generating three or more good candidates for each hire and getting 75% or more of all those offered a job to accept the job. We might also say that the "job fit" would be a good one, with 75% of those who accepted jobs still being in your employ after three years. Likewise, the failure attributes might be reflected by jobs open for an extended time, because good candidates were not found, or a high turnover rate in the first year after hire. Either way, we can see that the goal of the output attributes of the principal activity group is a choice of talented and motivated employees to hire, who do well in the job. The ability both to articulate that specific goal and to assign performance measures to its successful execution validates the designation of the principal activity group, because it describes a unique value add.

The development of outcome attributes for each principal activity group also defines the scientific basis for its future analysis and improvement, because it provides a means of evaluating the current effectiveness of creating that output through measures. In project management, these requirements will also reflect phase gates through which project continuation must pass.

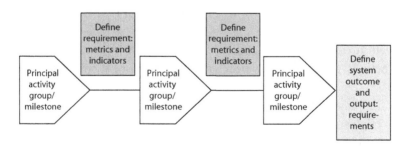

FIGURE 4.2
Showing the creation of outcome attributes associated with each principal activity group.

The outcome requirements for the entire system can then also be created in view of its stated business purpose, and these requirements statements may "borrow" from, or be the same as, some of the attributes you have created for each principal activity group. This is not a concern, and you should expect the outcome attributes of the entire system to mirror those of its individual components. This is synonymous with the experience of those practiced at root cause analysis, in which the repetition of a causation in different aspects of analysis underlines its importance in the overall solution. In the case of system science, we will need clear and measurable requirements statements to support the objective evaluation of each cycle of system performance and to support learning and continuous improvement, using both metrics and indicators.

5

Defining the Influencing Factors

The engine driving system science is the identification of the *influencing factors* of each principal activity group, and that is the next step in the creation of a system map.* Influencing factors should represent the planned actions that will positively influence best outputs of the system, and in documenting them, we are also documenting our achievable best practice operational plan.

Influencing factors could include key processes, although your process mapping and improvement should be a separate activity. In system mapping, you should simply name any key process encountered and show its placement in the overall system without showing its entire map. In this way, we can preserve the simplicity of the system map while still showing an important interdependency with process management.

The system map is looking at the operation of a single system as its focus and positively influencing its many factors to achieve its defined outcome. And while a key process may either add a significant part of its value or provide significant inputs to its operation, there will be many other activities, actions, and risks that are necessary to map and understand before you can develop a system operations plan to achieve its defined outcome and to overcome its numerous intervening variables. To best reflect its operational configuration, a completed system map will look like Figure 5.1.

So while we temporarily leave the treatment of intervening variables and risks to a future chapter, we will now look exclusively at the development of influencing factors. This effort will begin with cause and effect diagramming.

---

* If used for project management, we will represent the principal activity groups as milestones or phase gates, and the development of influencing factors will provide insight for risk management, project control, and quality assurance.

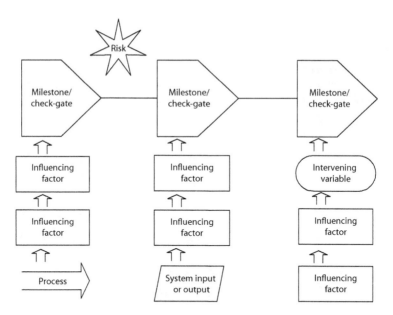

FIGURE 5.1

Completed system map. Shows "risk" star on top and principal activity groups.

Those familiar with cause and effect may know that it is often referred to as "asking 'why' five times" and that it is an effort to look for the root cause of a thing (the desired "effect") by asking why it happens and why each stated "why" happens. In short, it is the disaggregation of a complex causation into its component parts until a root cause is discovered. The "root" cause is a point where a person or group can best influence the most positive result. The same will hold true for identification of the influencing factors of a system.

In this specific use, the "effect" becomes the objective of each primary activity group as defined through its requirements of successful outcome. Its many causes can then be determined through brainstorming and further refined through analysis and testing. So your first development of a system map, and its influencing factors, should be later tested and improved using experimentation and feedback data over time.*

The use of cause and effect in this activity may be difficult to grasp at first, because for many years it has been used almost exclusively to identify the "root cause" of problems rather than as a means of engineering positive control factors, as it was first created by Kaoru Ishikawa. In his first English language book, *What Is Total Quality Control?*, Dr. Ishikawa

---

* See the Four Phases of Process and System Management in Figure 3.1.

said that the "effect" in a cause and effect diagram should be a "quality characteristic." He noted that the "cause factors must be controlled to obtain better products and effects. This approach anticipates problems and prevents them,"* a practice that he called "vanguard control."

Dr. Ishikawa also noted: "While there are many cause factors, the truly important ones, the cause factors which will sharply influence effects, are not many ... All we have to do is standardize two or three of the most important cause factors and control them. But first these important cause factors must be found."

The development of influencing factors can be accomplished through brainstorming cause factors and then analyzing the relative importance and impact of each. As with all kinds of brainstorming, many factors might be developed, including some obvious and simplistic ones such as "enough staff" and "enough time." It should be the system manager's job to find and list those touch points that are determinants of the specific value in that activity area and that are within the span of control (or influence) of that group. By again using the term *root cause*, we remind ourselves that we are seeking a point of primary influence on the activity area we have identified.

If a large group of such steps and actions is developed, it may be advisable to put them on a whiteboard and complete an inter-relationship analysis. In this exercise, it is necessary to simply ask "what drives what?" and to add an arrow from the step or action that is the "driver" to the step or action that is "driven." Then count the "out" arrows from each item, and be sure to designate those with the greatest impact as the principal "influencing factors" on your map.[†]

The questions sometimes associated with a force field analysis[‡] provide another useful technique, which is the development of influencing factors. So for each identified factor, you should ask: "What drives success in this activity?" and "What are the inhibitors of success in this activity?" In this manner, you are creating a system operation plan that is specific down to its influencing factors. The response to these questions will frame a definition of the steps and actions that will drive success in each influencing

---

* Ishikawa, Karou, 1985. *What Is Total Quality Control?* Prentice Hall, pp. 63–64.

† Brassard, Michael and Ritter, Diane, 2016. *The Memory Jogger 2: Tools for Continuous Improvement and Effective Planning.* GOAL/QPC Publishers. www.goalqpc.com.

‡ Force field analysis is an analytic method that identifies the forces and factors in place that support (or drive) the solution of an issue or problem and those that restrain or prevent its successful implementation. *The Memory Jogger 2: Tools for Continuous Improvement and Effective Planning,* GOAL/QPC, pp. 86–90. www.goalqpc.com.

factor and then in its associated principal activity group. That will make the choice of your influencing factors much more important. Only the most significant factors should be recorded on your system map.

Influencing factors may also be outputs, either of key processes or of other program or executive offices (other systems). Regardless, because those inputs have a large impact on the success of your defined systems, it may be highly relevant to establish supplier requirements and to attempt to influence the timely delivery of high-quality inputs as a means of better management of the performance of your own system. This will be another part of your specific system operation plan and one that you will later want to track through the development of feedback metrics and indicators. As with principal activity groups, you will find that the mapping and selection of influencing factors will be a learning experience for you and your work group and will help you to understand the best points of your management control for greatest system success.

It is noted that the influencing factors are designated with upward arrows as a representation of that influence on the principal activity group, not to suggest that they are successive or presented as a process flow.

Looking again at our human resources example, we might take the "On-boarding, placement, and orientation" activity group and put that on a cause and effect diagram. We would assume, of course, that we were looking for causes of "best possible practice" within that area, and if we did, our diagram might look like Figure 5.2.

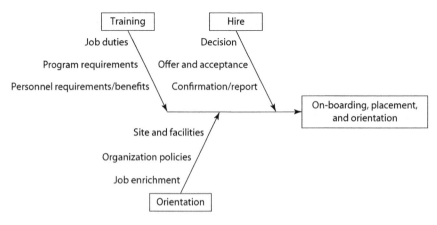

FIGURE 5.2
Fishbone diagram with "training" and "hire" boxes on top.

Some may argue that both the principal activity groups noted in the figure and their influencing factors could be flow-charted, and perhaps some specific applications of each could be flow-charted. But the system management approach deliberately does not focus on a specific application or a specific, closely defined set of deliverables. In this case, it is considering the workflow as being open to ALL the possible program variables and many different types of outputs—hires in this case.* So while a process flow would best be used to hire a specific group of positions under a specific set of conditions, a system map would be well suited to design the common best practice attributes of many different types of hires over a year or more. The system map should provide an overall management tool for practices necessary for all hires and for all human resource activities in the year. The system map will then necessarily embrace many important executive management activities that a process map will miss.

So for many system maps, and many principal activity groups, the influencing factors could be much broader. If we were going to map the system of strategic planning, for example, and it was decided that a determination of organizational strengths and weaknesses was the first principal activity group, then the influencing factors might include:

- Obtain executive perspectives on opportunities and threats
- Obtain program manager inputs on strengths and weaknesses
- Review performance metrics against goals/analysis of trends
- Develop market and customer analysis
- Develop analysis and alternatives
- Obtain consensus and decisions
- Align objectives and tactics

All of these factors may be important, although the specific means of achieving each would be highly variable and would likely depend on "intervening variables." So the specific methods for each that are selected from year to year will likely vary significantly based on the preference of the leaders involved, the economic (or political) conditions, and the time available. And depending on the assigned importance of strategic planning to the executive leadership in any given year, its system mapping

---

* System management uses the term *object of value creation* to reflect that a single system (unlike a single process) may produce many different versions of its outputs over time. This is perhaps best illustrated by a system of project management used by a project management office, which would have very high variance in projects while still following the same system "best practices," including checklists, reports, templates, standard methods, and guidelines.

might benefit from sub-system analysis or perhaps from greater design and standardization.

The science of system management does follow predictable rules, but it is malleable, based on circumstances, resources, level of importance, and other special factors. Our job as system managers is to try to standardize and to allow learning based on performance feedback over time, and that depends on the definition of principal activity groups and influencing factors. So at its first completion, a system map might look like Figure 5.3.

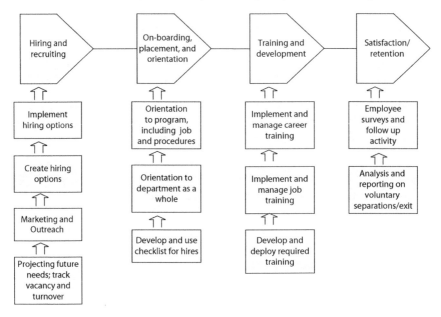

FIGURE 5.3
Providing a capable and motivated workforce.

Those familiar with process mapping should see many differences. First, a system map differs from a process map in that there is not just one exclusive path that represents an output cycle, and that is not the purpose of a system map. It represents the best practices and continuous action for an executive leader or a program office.*

System mapping is not designed as a guide to individual process actions. So while process maps are specific to a course of actions to deliver specific outputs, system maps show the actions of management to best achieve a group of outputs.

---

* Alternately, the system mapping of a project path could well show chronological milestones and could, in fact, be mapped as sequential actions. This is discussed in Chapter 9.

6

Defining Metrics and Indicators for Your System Map

One of the greatest benefits of system maps is the need to define requirements both for principal activity groups and for any of the influencing
factors that are deemed important to best outcomes. The definition of such
requirements allows leaders to obtain feedback in the form of metrics and
indicators and to use that information to understand its current capability
and to chart future improvements. It will add to the system operational
plan, because it will show what it is designed to achieve, where there is
error and rework, and where it can improve. So while the first version
of this plan will show current best known practice, it will also point to
a new achievable best practice for your system. The foundation for these
next-level improvements is the development of metrics and indicators that
correspond to principal activity groups and to influencing factors.

Metrics are defined as numeric values that express performance levels
comparatively and relative to a scale of possible performance. They are like
grades on an academic report card that reflect how well you performed on
exams and assignments. Their relative ranking expresses average, good,
and bad performance, and they can be easily compared with others.

Most of the time, when managers begin to discuss "performance measurement," they immediately seek to put as many aspects of performance
as possible on such a comparative scale, which is both difficult and likely
to breed fear in those judged and distortions of reports to ensure positive
results. Performance metrics are discouraged in system mapping, since
systems are often not under the direct control of any one person or group
and are subject to numerous intervening variables. In this sense, the use
of performance metrics alone to influence positive results is futile and
counter-productive. When metrics are found to be most relevant, they

should be viewed as evidence of what has happened and not as a means of providing positive or negative feedback to your work group or any individual within it. While metrics are important, in the context of system mapping they should be used simply to learn current performance and to test the impact of changes designed to improve performance.

More important are indicators, defined as data or information that shows whether a goal or planned performance level was achieved. Indicators are checklist items or actions that are expected to be 100% complete, and they are often more important than metrics in several ways. First, indicators can and should be designed as leading or predictive actions that are fundamental to achieving excellent outputs. So if we reference our just-created system map for "providing a capable and motivated workforce" (see Figure 5.3), we can begin to define the checklist actions that will define success in each of our influencing factors.

In this cited example, we might find that "projecting future needs, tracking vacancy and turnover" would depend on quarterly updates and analysis of vacancy and turnover reports and meetings with all program managers to understand needs. Either or both of these things can be put on a checklist, and 100% completion of all checklist items can be used as our indicator.

In this sense, we can see that the development of actions that pair with indicators can, in many cases, build and support the best achievable management practices that are our goal.

In using system management, you will find that management's ability to influence results is based on following up and providing feedback on the completion of key actions that ensure success. So, through the establishment of influencing factors *that define that success*, and creating indicators to give visibility to effective completion, we build a system operational plan. In effect, we are identifying our "points of control" as managers, through which we will ensure the success of our principal activity groups and our intended business purpose.

As another example, let's look at the System of Strategic Planning (see Chapter 5, in a bulleted list preceding Figure 5.3). We can assume that one influencing factor of "determination of organizational strengths and weaknesses." We can then set an indicator (or series of checklist items) as "scheduling and completing interviews with chief executives to develop strengths and weaknesses by March 1" and another as "consolidating a statement of planning strengths and weaknesses by March 31." Then we will have developed a means of feedback on key factors driving system success and a plan for system operation.

Metrics on overall strategic planning outcomes may be harder to achieve and less attributable to specific causation, since organizational success may be due only in part to the strategic plan. Regardless, excellent strategic planning may influence success, and having indicators regarding the completion of best practice "influencing factors" will provide leading measures of success and will define the necessary path to get there.

DEFINING INTERVENING VARIABLES AND RISK

While influencing factors are going to define the proactive management strategies for system operation, it is the intervening variables and risks that can interrupt or completely thwart hoped-for objectives. While there are many similarities between the two, this text will refer to *intervening variables* as factors within the defined organizational system or operational context and *risks* as factors outside the span of control of the defined system and its context.

Intervening variables, then, can be defined as known or likely changes in system map assumptions, constraints, outcome requirements, resources, and schedule. Risks will be disruptive events and unexpected or unplanned circumstances to which the system must respond. In the case of intervening variables, then, we can use scenario planning. In the case of risks, we must use risk assessment and risk management. The completion of a plan for both is important, since the objective of system science is to obtain a predictable and reliable outcome from a defined (and mapped) system.

So, for example, in the strategic planning system map, a typical intervening variable might be a special initiative imposed mid-course by the executive or the governing board of the organization. The proper response would be to prepare a scenario analysis in which one or more "best" responses would be developed in advance of the event, so that a rational and feasible plan for that event is already in existence.

A similar strategy would need to be developed for risks, and the use of the project risk management standard of the project management body of knowledge (PMBOK)* is one recognized means. It is important to note that system risks (just like project risks) have multiple causes and multiple effects. So after system risks have been identified and scored for likelihood and impact, an analysis of those causes and effects should be conducted. In building your system operational plan, then, the actions necessary to either prevent or detect risk occurrence can be developed and included. Strategies for responding to risks that do occur and become real problems can then also be completed.

In either case, the development of plans that anticipate and respond to the most likely intervening variables and risks is an essential part of system management and promotes consistent and reliable results.

---

* *A Guide to the Project Management Body of Knowledge*, PMBOK Guide, Project Management Institute. www.pmi.org ANSI/PMI 99-001-2013.

7

Application of the System Management Standard

The focused work associated with what you have done in the first six chapters of this book should have now led you to define an important, or "key," system over which you have control or significant influence and to do some detailed analysis of its purpose and the factors that drive its success. In effect, you should have defined and "deployed" a mental model*
of your system, your first-version operational plan! You should also now have developed some kind of analysis of its result and where its deficiencies may be.

This chapter will explain the system management standard, which provides a framework against which to evaluate your current system and its operation and a means of identifying other aspects of its control and improvement that you may want to include. The first basic aspects are a definition of what you want your system to produce and a measurable standard of that output. These are enhanced by including a business purpose (a "mission statement" of business purpose) and a name. In finalizing that high-level system statement, you should have also looked back to your organizational mission and its strategic plan to ensure that your chosen system is in alignment with the organizational purpose and direction. If there are any specific organizational goals for the defined area you are seeking to improve, or "system scope," you should be able to see how your defined system will help you to achieve those goals, and the goals should be reflected in defined system outputs. You should have also identified interdependencies with other business units (aka "systems") that may

---

* Ultimately, the creation of structured and designed systems is done through a "logos," or mental model, which is the product of a leader, or a group of leaders, either formal or informal. It is first a product of thought.

provide inputs to your systems, and each of these handoff points presents an opportunity for future improvement.

Beyond that, you should have created principal activity groups representing the knowledge, skill, and ability groups that create specific value add, which is necessary for your system output and outcome.* Each principal activity group that you have defined must have attributes of its successful completion and even performance measures (metrics and indicators) to evaluate your level of success in each area.

You should have produced at least one cause and effect diagram of *each* principal activity group and decided which of those causes (influencing factors) significantly contribute to your success in that activity group. As with all cause and effect exercises, revisiting and improving your first effort will build better analytic results. You can and should obtain stakeholder feedback and performance metrics, where available, to enhance your analysis of influencing factors, and force field analysis of what drives and inhibits success in each area may also provide significant knowledge that will build your system operational plan. It is also possible that your system analysis will identify key processes that are primarily responsible for value creation within principal activity areas, and those are possible future targets for Lean process improvement activity.[†]

The system mapping activity described here includes defining and structuring a key system and beginning its standardization and improvement. The first significant realization here is that you are creating a mental model, or "logos," and that is at the heart of system management! It is a decision of will and consciousness to bring about a different result in the world or to make the world a better place in some way. While the examples we have presented, that is, the purpose of a program office, most often "human resources," is not overly broad, the system model can in fact be used to develop a structured system map of "neighborhood crime reduction" as well as for "organizational decision-making." Its application is boundless, and through definition of systems, sub-systems, and processes, it will allow a thinker (or "leader") to structure the forces within a span of control or influence to achieve better results.

---

* Systems, unlike processes, are not as focused on outputs as on outcomes. Even though most systems will have a set of outputs, they are generally valued primarily for the outcome produced. Both outputs and outcomes are therefore important for tracking, evaluating, and improving systems.

† A beginning point for process evaluation is the application of the ASQ Government Division process maturity standard, available online at: http://asq.org/gov/ in the quality information section.

Part of this equation, then, is to create aligned thinking and to access the knowledge and resources of all those you can reach in line with your system goals. This is done by first creating a "best known" system practice and then defining an "achievable best practice." The "best known" practice will often require that you access the knowledge and experience of stakeholders both in and outside of your organization. This is similar to the process of "leveling" that is described in the literature of process management and improvement, in which a work group team may be assembled to discuss a process or the nature of problems or to brainstorm possible improvements. However it is done, reaching out for different points of view will strengthen your mental model, your system map, your system approach, and ultimately, its deployment.

System management will also follow the Define, Measure, Analyze, Improve, and Control (DMAIC) model of Lean process improvement and will benefit from cycles of improvement. So you will define, measure, analyze, improve, and control a system in the same manner as for a process. This is noted in Figure 7.1, where the replacement of the word "process" by the word "system" makes the model entirely applicable (Figure 7.1).

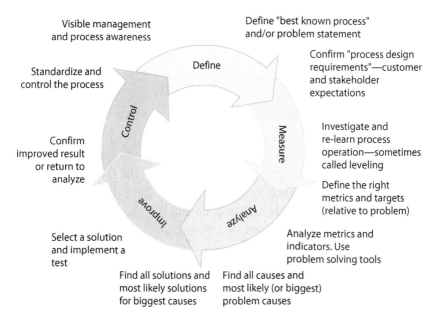

FIGURE 7.1
Define, Measure, Analyze, Improve, Control.

A standardized toolset for evaluating your system maturity is found in the system management standard, which has been professionally reviewed and adopted by the American Society for Quality Government Division.* This standard is based on the idea that quality processes and systems (together referred to as *workflows*) should create excellent work continuously and predictably. This is what is referred to as the *capability* of a process or system.

The method of achieving a consistent and continuous flow of error-free work is to prevent the occurrence of problems by building quality principles (sometimes referred to as *quality assurance* and *quality control*) into the operational process. So for example, once a best known practice work flow is devised, it is management's job to ensure that it is followed. Continuous improvement of your system should then be possible through periodic review and revision of your system approach and deployment using the following standard.

SYSTEM MANAGEMENT STANDARD—SUMMARY VERSION

The system management standard is measured through the evaluation of four criteria areas, including

1. System purpose and structure
2. Goal directedness
3. Management of intervening variables and risk
4. Alignment, evaluation, and improvement

The following summary table is an excerpt from the entire system management standard, which is available online at the web address noted in the footnote.† An obvious benefit of application of the standard is the ability to score and rank a set of systems throughout an organization, both as

---

* Government Division has taken the lead in developing measurable systems and process standards, because it does not have the forces of competition or consumer preference to drive an interest in quality, and in the final analysis, it may have to rely on quality "audit." Regardless, the principles of system management apply to all economic activity.

† The system management standard is available online at: http://www.asq.org/gov in the quality information section.

a means of evaluation and improvement and as a means of planning for future improvement.

The following tables show the progression of each scoring criteria area, from a numeric score of 0–5, with the largest number reflecting the greatest system maturity. This mirrors the scoring models used for many surveys, in which "strong agreement" is typically at the highest level, and "strong disagreement" is typically at the lowest. In this case, the highest scoring is reserved for the highest conformance to best practice, and the level of conformance is called *system maturity*.

Using this standard, the maturity of systems can be ranked from a score of 0–20—or as a percentage of all points possible. A summary of the system management criteria is provided in Table 7.1.

TABLE 7.1

System Management Standard—Simplified

Systems Purpose and Structure

0   The system is named and has known purpose, but no structure. Specific system actions, events, and activities respond to outside influences and may be based on political agendas or individual judgments, without regard to analysis or past learning experience.

5   There is documented evidence of an ordered system that delivers uniform and predictable quality outputs over multiple operational cycles. The ordered system is supported by a system map and supporting documented covering all tasks, accountabilities, and contributing factors. Major intervening variables and system risks have been identified. The system map links to process maps as necessary, to accomplish organizational goals. Requirements statements for process inputs or outputs are built into systems requirements. System deployment is specific to the means used to manage the system and to ensure its continuing operations according to design. Operational deployment is supported by responsibilities and accountability for each contributing resource group, and through the use of indicators and performance measures for all principal activity groups. There is evidence of the use of this system management structure for three or more years.

Goal Directedness through Measures and Feedback

0   The system has no clearly defined outcomes, and no expectations for its performance. Its hoped-for outcomes are ambiguous.

5   Performance feedback and objective measures are linked to this system and all its defined activity groups. Positive levels and trends exist for the entire system and for all its principal activities. Several indicators and measures are available for each defined activity group. There is evidence that the performance of this defined system has improved and contributed to improving organizational outcomes over 3 or more years.

(Continued)

TABLE 7.1 (CONTINUED)

System Management Standard—Simplified

Management of Intervening Variables and Risk

0   Intervening variables and risk have not been identified or are unknown.

5   The risk management plan is analyzed and reviewed at least annually. System design and structure have been modified to lessen the impact or occurrence of intervening variable and risks. There is documented evidence of the use of analysis to lessen risk and system impacts. Root cause analysis is used to design risk management plans. There is documented evidence of systems learning and improvement.

Alignment, Evaluation, and Improvement

0   There are no systematic efforts to learn and improve. The resources and personnel that constitute the system do not recognize its existence.

5   There is evidence of continuous systematic annual improvement, participated in by all defined systems personnel. Responsibilities, accountability, consultation, and informing roles have been identified for each primary activity group, and for dependent tasks and activities. There are measurable, positive results on outcomes, and in each activity group, with demonstrated positive relationship to all dependent processes.

System purpose and structure refers to whether the purpose or "aim" of the system is recognized and documented, whether its hoped-for results (or "outputs") have been defined, and whether its approach and deployment are clear and used to ensure the intended results. There are lots of ways that systems in organizations can suffer, and two of the most crippling are the failure to clearly define why they exist and what they are intended to accomplish.

While it sounds hard to believe that either of those two things could exist, they do. Picture an accounting office, whose job in a native system (lacking design) may be envisioned to be paying the bills, depositing receipts, and balancing the books. The focus on those things alone may allow a sloppiness in, say, the coding of payments and receipts, so even though we know the books are balanced, we do not get good information reports on who is spending and on what, or on where revenue is coming from and why. Many important factors, such as the accounting office interactions with the people who spend or provide receivables, with external auditors, and with information technology systems design may all be invisible or relegated to the category of "unimportant detail." This is not unimportant detail but essential detail that results in vast consequences and unintended complexity and inefficiency, for which the organization will pay a price.

The creation of a system approach and its deliberate deployment are therefore critical and important aspects of system management, which are recognized in the system purpose and structure category area.

Goal directedness builds on the definition of hoped-for system results and outputs and asks whether metrics and indicators (collectively called *measures*) are linked to either the principal activity areas, the influencing factors, or the attributes of successful performance of the activity areas or the system as a whole. In other words, have we created focused attention on objective and measurable attributes of system success, and are we using that ongoing performance feedback to understand what works and what does not and to develop continuous improvement? The goal directedness criterion provides the measurement component of systems, which allows DMAIC and Lean to work.

Management of intervening variables and risk asks whether those factors that are most likely to disrupt the optimal system design plan have been identified and addressed. The identification of the intervening variables and risks is best done through an annual review in which their likelihood and consequences are documented in a risk register. This category asks whether risk management strategies for each significant category have been created. Root cause analysis is then used to evaluate whether prevention or mitigation can be built into the system design. Where risks must be accepted, a prepared scenario analysis may be used to respond. This category emphasizes the need to evaluate the factors of system disruption and how prevention, mitigation, or response is built into its operating plan.

Alignment, evaluation, and improvement asks to see whether the system goes through annual evaluation, improvement, and change to reflect learning gained through its structured review. This criterion then looks at whether those who run the system refer to and use the system map, its performance measures, and its operational plan. This evaluation category asks to see how deployment occurs, whether those responsible and accountable for each principal activity group have been defined, and how their actions and oversight are held in conformance with a deployment plan. It also looks to see a history of evaluation, review, and improvement. In effect, it holds systems accountable to cycles of continuous improvement.

The system management standard and its four category areas provide an important tool for evaluating the maturity of a system. This maturity score is in itself a predictive or "leading" measure of the quality that is likely to be achieved. Through the definition and standardization of achievable best practices, and including a set of indicators and metrics associated with those practices, you will be ensuring the defined result. The honest evaluation of system maturity will make your quality practice visible and will hold everyone accountable for the completion of defined tasks. It will also provide a roadmap based on criteria items that are *not* currently satisfied, and future steps and actions that will further your system performance.

8

The Overlap of System and Process Management

As noted in Chapter 5, we should expect some key processes to align within each defined system, especially when using system mapping in the context of a program office. This will be true because managers will intuitively try to define and standardize processes in some manner when there is high repetition and high value. It may be entirely new to realize, though, that systems often provide either inputs to processes or require outputs from processes, and are therefore its "customers."* Figure 8.1 is provided as an example of that relationship.

The realization that systems *are* inputs and outputs to processes is important to practitioners of Lean process improvement, since these actions are often the source of wait time to process flow and are sometimes reflective of the kind of business-necessary non-value add process steps that Lean seeks to minimize or eliminate. Indeed, many of the requirements of process steps are defined by business systems, which can now themselves be investigated for value add and non-value added activity. By inserting system management into a structured realm of quality analysis and quality improvement, we will set up a new analytic framework to positively change these results.

The input and output from systems to process and back again should not be a surprise, because one definition of a system is a set of resources under the direct and/or indirect span of control of a leader or leadership

---

* In a highly structured quality organization, there will be great benefit from allowing process owners to establish "customer" requirements for system inputs that are required for production and applying metrics to those inputs. Likewise, system managers can establish requirements for process outputs and track the performance of delivery in the same manner.

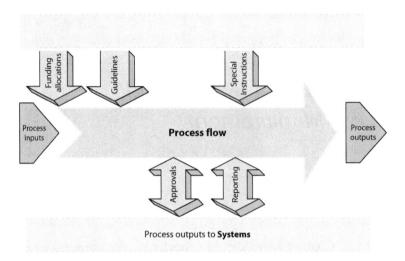

FIGURE 8.1
System inputs to process.

group and charged to produce a defined result. As noted in our presentation of the Unifying Theory of Work Management, the overall objective of management should always be to define best known management practice, define best achievable management practice, standardize the means of providing the best achievable practice, and define the points of control for that practice. This same method will apply equally to systems and process, and in fact, process is an important sub-group of system management.

Process management, or "science," must differ from system management, or "science," because of the features noted in Table 2.1. To summarize, the better precision of process science is possible because its defined outputs are generally in high volume, with specific standard requirements, and are often produced by a dedicated work team in a controlled environment. Systems, on the other hand, often produce various outputs with variable and changing requirements, do not have a dedicated work team, and are produced outside of a single manager's span of control.* This is illustrated in Figure 8.2.

---

* Systems in the larger world, such as crime prevention and control, can be expected to be somewhat outside the span of control even of the organization (a police department in this case) charged with their control.

Process/system types

High frequency **Low variation**	**High frequency** **High variation**
(of tasks/methods/output)	(of tasks/methods/output)
PROCESS Licensing actions Benefit determinations Routine program action	SYSTEM or PROCESS Legal actions Accident investigations IT help desk
Low frequency **Low variation**	**Low frequency** **High variation**
(of tasks/methods/output)	(of tasks/methods/output)
SYSTEM or PROCESS Capital needs analysis Design/construct civil Contract actions	SYSTEMS Strategic plan New technology projects HR recruitments

FIGURE 8.2
4-Section grid—"High frequency low variation" at top left.

It is important to realize that the greater the variation in the process output (what we can call the *object of value creation*) and the less control there is over the environment in which it occurs, the less effective process science will be as a primary management strategy. So consider, for example, the following processes:

- The issuance of a monthly parking pass at a government service counter has specificity of both what is produced (a single type of parking pass) and the environment in which it is created (the same employees in a specific office).
- Residential curbside garbage collection has a standard truck collecting standardized garbage cans but on very dissimilar streets and principal residency types. There is high similarity of service but great variation in how the standard service must be delivered.
- Police patrol activities have similarly trained officers, identically equipped, driving standard patrol cars, but then applying widely varying services in a wide variety of environments. There is great dissimilarity in services provided and in the environment in which they are delivered.

As you may conclude, the ease of application of standard process management tools diminishes greatly as we move from monthly parking pass issuance to police patrol activities, and the need to apply system management techniques increases proportionately. One way this has been expressed in the existing management literature is through the presentation of the difference between scientific and artistic process (as in the article, "When Should a Process Be Art, Not Science?").* This article states that "[t]here are some processes that naturally resist definition and standardization—that are more art than science," and it correctly asserts that different management practices should then be adopted. As examples, it mentions leadership training, auditing, hedge fund management, customer service, software development, account relationship management, business development, and industrial design.

The article notes that this is "judgment-based work, craft-work, or professional work," which must have "variation in the process, its inputs, and its outputs." It states that the traditional process management approach (which it refers to as "scientific") attempts to "bring the environment under control ... [and] impose complex rules that spell out what to do in every possible circumstance." In contrast, the article suggests that broad, thematic guidance allows employees to use judgment and improvise. "If a process is artistic, invest in giving employees the skills, judgment, and cultural appreciation to excel in variable conditions." And it also suggests an emphasis on story-telling among employees, the use of lessons learned, and customer-focused feedback.

This book, of course, suggests that the development of principal activity groups and their influencing activities will provide a better and more objective basis for the "cultural appreciation" of the story-telling and learning that must occur. It will also guide leaders to develop achievable best practices through development of indicators for influencing factors and system operational plans that carry out those practices. System operational plans will include procedures, templates, milestones, guides, standards, and other bodies of knowledge that reflect best practice expectations and organizational knowledge. Regardless, it is important to be able to recognize that such artistic steps are now embedded in many key processes. These exist wherever leadership approvals, legal review, and other kinds of professional "sufficiency" review are required.

Where each of these steps exists, the development of the attributes of success or of failure in the step will help to ferret out measurable attributes and indicators that will lead to greater success and less delay. Indicators will reflect checklists to make visible the regular use and completion of the best practices outlined in the best practice operational plan. This may

---

* Hall, J.M. and Johnson, M.E., 2009. *Harvard Business Review*, March, pp. 58–65.

reduce fear of failure and speed decisions. Regardless, the ability to identify a so-called artistic process, or a process step as a system or system step, will improve its best management.

Both process science and system science seek to create uniform and predictable outputs and outcomes, but there are significant differences in the nature of the workflows they represent. In conjunction with the American Society for Quality Government Division, the author has developed the process management standard* and the system management standard†as a source of reference for each. And while there is a great body of literature regarding process management and process science, the resources for system management are few and generally fragmentary.

Recognized professional problem areas in the practice of process science are perhaps most important to the new science of system management, because they show us where currently known practice does not work well, and lead us to new possible solutions through system science. One of the most important of these is the area of "networked steps," which could also be called *interdependent value creation.* Networked steps must exist where the criteria of the process step are creative or subjective, or deductive, or where the value added is a standard of judgment—hopefully professional judgment! Figure 8.3 shows what a networked step may look like.

To better understand, we might imagine the Western pioneers on the American frontier deciding in which direction to travel. In this case, we know there must be one best possible decision, but the available information to make that decision is insufficient. The only alternative is for the most knowledgeable parties to offer theories, test each other's theories,

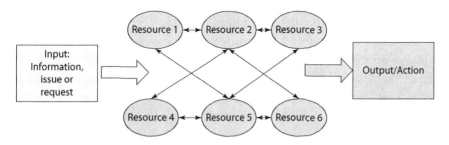

FIGURE 8.3
Showing networked process or system activities.

---

* The process management standard is not specifically covered in this book, but is available online at: http://asq.org/gov in the quality information section.

† A summary version of the system management standard is presented in Table 7.1, and a current and complete copy is available online at: http://www.asq.org/gov in the quality information section.

and then select the best one—the one that seems most plausible. We can see, then, that networked steps may involve building a shared knowledge, applying available knowledge, decision-making, or all three. Likewise, if a growing business contacts a state governor's office and asks what services may be available if they relocate to that state, there may be a similar multi-party discussion, and likely over a period of time.

A variant of networked steps is found in associative steps, which do not have to be processed by a group but can be practiced by just one person acting alone—perhaps by running a series of tests or diagnostics. If the number and order of tests or diagnostics have just one recommended path, process mapping will best apply. But if the number and order of tests use professional judgment, system mapping will best apply.

So in healthcare, a nurse may have a variable set of communications and tests they will run on each patient to determine their status and any potential needs. The tests may be as simple as saying "hello" or as complex as checking blood pressure, but the thought of a single prescriptive process would be impossible.

A system model will be preferable in all of these examples, because a single best path for action with specific steps and requirements cannot be devised. Even if each of these scenarios were repeated multiple times, the "best practice" path devised would have to be interpretive, based on specifics of the situations that would have changed from the last time. Clearly, system science is the better model, as presented in the earlier chapters of this book. However, it is also possible that a key process you map may have just a single networked step, which makes process mapping still the preferred practice. Regardless, we can break out the networked step in a system map so that the two disciplines work together!

Another example found in healthcare is that of associative determinations, where it was learned that the steps necessary to discharge a patient from the hospital were both iterative and interdependent. Patient discharge is often called a process, but one healthcare process team found that its process mapping efforts were not helpful and resulted only in a series of inter-connected and interdependent determinations and actions that were impossible to manage in sequence.* As a result, a checklist method was developed around the three categorical areas noted in Table 8.1.

---

* Example provided by Maine General Medical Center, at the Lean Systems Summit, 2015. Thanks to Debbie Karter, MSN, BSN, RN and her team, who developed this work management system. Team members included Kevin Lane, Jessica Nalesnik, Rabun Dodge, Elizabeth Kingsbury, and Patricia Morini.

TABLE 8.1

Tasks to Clear/Complete for Discharge

Physician (MD)	Stable/positive condition
	No symptoms (24 hours)
	Meds/replacement for IVs
	Oxygen orders
Nurse (RN)	LBM—digestive function ok
	IV meds removed
	Mobility needs met
	Feeding/nutrition
	Medication education
Care Management (CM)	Discharge destination
	Home equipment available
	Transportation
	Further services in place
	Insurance prior authorization

The physician was asked to see whether their patients had positive health indicators, the registered nurses reviewed current patient indicators, and the "care management" team made sure the patient was going to an adequate home location, had transportation, and had provided the hospital with insurance information. Each group of criteria were reviewed in a standing meeting each morning to see whether all criteria were met (Table 8.1).

The evaluation of readiness for discharge is then completed on a checklist (see Table 8.2), with a "ready" or "not ready" indicator being provided

TABLE 8.2

Checklist: Evaluation of Patient Readiness for Discharge

Room #	Date	Physician Requirements	Nurse Requirements	Payments, Transport, Outpatient Care
100	today	×	×	✓
101	today	✓	✓	×
102	today	✓	×	×
103	today	×	×	×
104	today	×	✓	✓
105	today	×	✓	✓
106	today	✓	✓	✓

Note: × means not fulfilled; ✓ means fulfilled.

by a representative of each group as noted. Each group completes its review with appropriate professional standards. Again, this workflow is clearly not a process, because there is no one prescribed path to achieve it.

It should be noted that the requirements of each of the groups used in this example are professional standards, which in their actual application are largely subjective rather than objective and strictly measurable. The "checklist" evaluation and review method devised by this team provides an excellent model for other similar types of system management or for the management of system steps within processes.

The concept of multiple and subjective professional standards being used as requirements for the satisfactory completion of system requirements is discussed further in the next chapter. These will be referred to as multidimensional project performance indicators. As the name implies, it is a clear overlap between system management and project management and, again, proves the continuity of these management practices.

9

The Overlap of System and Projects

As we noted in Chapter 2, one project by itself will never be repeated. It is unique. But the team members who plan and deliver projects, the business units managing projects, and the body of knowledge used by an organization for its project management will continue with future projects in a cyclic fashion. For this reason, system management is a natural fit.

There are many other reasons why projects respond very well to a system management structure. One predominant reason is that systems and projects must deliver end products that are multifaceted and have many requirements. So, for example, a "delivered" water treatment plant must have multiple buildings and processing facilities, pumps, filters, treatment tanks, valves, gauges, and even instructional manuals for the staff who will operate them. In addition, projects of all kinds must frequently respond to modifications of output requirements as they are delivered due to feedback, testing of deliverables, and shortages of time or budget. They must accommodate the many change orders that will be presented.

In other words, the object of value creation is really many objects, each with many specific delivery criteria. The purpose of the sum of all these objects of value creation is a working thing—a wastewater treatment plant—that is described in terms of a business purpose, or "aim."

The delivery criteria for our project (aka "system") may have some acceptance criteria that are measurable and specific, but many others may be subjective and evaluated only through either a "reasonable person" standard or a professional standard (in other words, is this acceptable in the eyes of our subject matter experts?).

For these reasons, project managers will never be able to define single specific paths for the delivery of a project, and their primary means of learning and improvement will include both models and templates, forms and guides, and lessons learned. To the reader of this book, these should all sound very familiar by now as the same tools that we must use in system management. However, system management brings a powerful new tool for project managers in the form of system mapping and influencing factors.

One example of a project on a system map is shown in Figure 9.1. While this example has used the process management groups from the PMBOK* standard, it has also adapted at least the first two principal activity groups to reflect *some* of the criteria of successful completion of each, as described in the system mapping chapters. By asking the attributes of successful completion of each principal activity group ("process management group," in PMBOK terminology) and the attributes of failure in each, we are forcing a discussion of our project, what we need to accomplish, and the risks we face. This will then allow a robust discussion of influencing factors that will drive our success.

Keep in mind that depending on the nature of the project, we may want to make sub-system maps for any part of this effort so that we can better understand and control its component actions. So we may, for example,

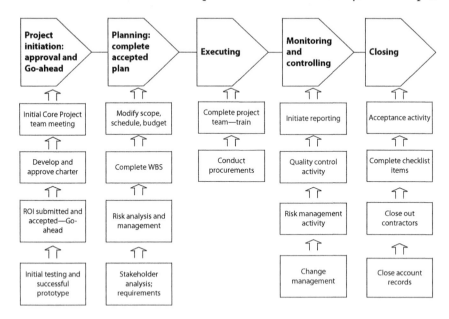

FIGURE 9.1
Project management on a system map.

---

* The Project Management Body of Knowledge (PMBOK), Project Management Institute.

want to make a sub-system map for work breakdown structure (WBS), through which we will have the managers of component parts provide activity, schedule, and resource requirements for their parts of the project. We may also choose to do force field analysis on that component to list the driving forces of success and the inhibitors. In short, we can see that the system mapping discipline offers the project manager many new tools!

Another possible application would be during the monitoring and controlling phase, when we may wish to develop a system map to reflect our milestones. If we did so, the principal activity groups could be arranged as shown in Figure 9.2.

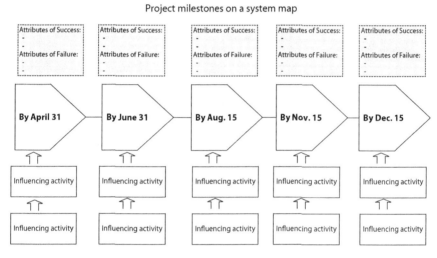

Project milestones on a system map

FIGURE 9.2
Sample system map with Attributes of Success and Attributes of Failure on top row.

MANAGING MULTI-PHASE PROJECTS

There are many possible applications of system mapping to process management, and one unique example comes from the California Department of Transportation, which is seeking to better manage the quality of delivered civil construction works, largely roads and bridges, through the use of a system map showing project initiation through construction. The system map shown in Figure 9.3 was developed.

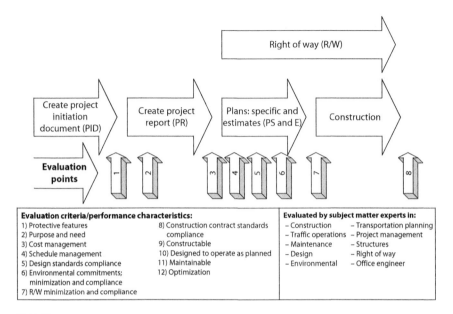

FIGURE 9.3
Quality management system for design product evaluation.

The system map presented in Figure 9.3 deviates from the model of this book in that it shows the overlap of primary program areas, which are depicted as processes, rather than principal activity groups, as is recommended. Regardless, the selection of evaluation areas did focus the group on defining criteria for success, which has allowed measured evaluation of its results.

This system mapping exercise was important to them for several reasons, most importantly because it maps the cooperative work of five different work units and shows the necessary handoffs of quality project documents and outputs between them all. Needless to say, the definition of high-quality project documents and outputs has been greatly debated in the past and has been seen as a primary cause of delay and poor results in the constructed project. There has been a clear need for uniform standards with acceptance criteria for handoff, and system mapping facilitated their effort.

Their interdisciplinary project management team consisted of nine core functional areas from project management, design, structure design, environmental, right of way, traffic operations, transportation planning, construction, and maintenance. Representation from the office of engineering and structure construction was also added to comment on the final design phase. The team developed the evaluation criteria performance characteristic groups shown in Figure 9.3 and subcategorized these into a series of specific individual performance criteria relevant to each group.

So for example, the design standards criteria include an evaluation of whether (and how well) the design

- Meets Highway Design Manual requirements
- Meets Design Informational Bulletin requirements
- Meets American Association of State Highway and Transportation Local Standard requirements
- Conforms to the Project Development Procedures Manual
- Meets the need for improvements to existing highway interchanges and local roads

Each of these criteria is scored on a 1–5 scale by a group of designated professional appraisers at each of the eight defined evaluation points, and low scores in any criteria at any point require response and remediation.

This application of system mapping is unique and important in several ways. First, it is providing leading measures of quality in the final project deliverables. Second, its rating scale provides what might be called *multidimensional performance indicators* provided by subject matter experts on a standardized scale and at pre-determined points. Even though professional judgment is admittedly subjective, the development of specific criteria standards and a uniform rating scale has made this a much more valid standard.

This system mapping has recognized that binding together interdependent work flows (any of which could arguably be called *processes*) is much better done through system mapping. Since, as noted in Chapter 8, many of these processes include networked steps, associative steps, and associative determinations, there is no one single path that can be standardized or followed, and attempts to do so will prove futile.

USE OF THE RESPONSIBLE, ACCOUNTABLE, CONSULTED, AND INFORMED (RACI) TOOL

In recognizing a shared identity between projects and systems, we may also conclude that there may be an opportunity to use project management tools very productively in system management. One such opportunity discovered by the author has been the use of RACI analysis to clarify the roles of individuals within larger organizations when a predictable and seamless handoff of process outputs across organizational boundaries is required.

In the cited instance, a state housing development funding organization was dependent on a series of handoffs within its business unit structure. These included the development of a notice of the availability of public funding for eligible housing development, receipt and scoring of applications for that funding, issuance of award letters, tracking of the close of contracts, monitoring of construction, underwriting long-term financing, and supervision and approval of final occupancy. Because there were many such award cycles initiated every year, and because each program cycle (from award to occupancy) could take multiple years, management had difficulty in tracking the many program cycles, which were all in various stages of completion. The number of such awards and limited staffing also made the appointment of a project manager for each one infeasible.

This organization needed an assured system of handoffs that existed below top management, was easy to track, and was certain in its execution. The organization selected the use of a RACI matrix* to define responsible, accountable, consulted and informed personnel at each major task group, defined on a system map. Most importantly, it was determined that there would be just one accountable (A) person responsible for the completion of each task group, and that the accountable party would act as a task group project manager and would check their work and progress versus a master schedule until done (Table 9.1).

Each accountable party was then held responsible for pulling together all the designated responsible parties (those who had to complete part of the task group work) into a mini-project team. The accountable party was also expected to obtain "go-ahead" affirmations from each designated "consulted" party and to inform all others of the defined activity. Where intervening variables or risks were encountered, the accountable party was asked to elevate the issues to executive management for resolution. In this way, a daisy-chain of handoffs was created, with accountable parties inputting achievements and affirmatively handing off to the next accountable party. This simple use of an established project management tool on

* From the Project Management Body of Knowledge: The definition of roles for each major activity group includes Responsible, Accountable, Consulted, Informed (RACI).

TABLE 9.1

Definitions for Terms—RACI Tool

Term	Meaning
Accountable (A)	The office and delegated person expected to be *driving and approving* the work done by responsible parties in this task group. The accountable will perform project management for this task group, and will elevate issues to higher authority if any insurmountable problem develops. Also expected to record completion and hand off complete work to the next-in-line accountable party.
Responsible (R)	Unit and designated individuals expected to *perform designated* tasks according to a performance standard. This work will be reviewed by the Accountable party for acceptance. Since a working team may be necessary to perform the work, the supervisor or designated lead will deliver required deliverables at the direction of the Accountable person at that point in time.
Consulted (C)	Work units from whom opinions are necessary and sought, based on two-way communication. It is expected that consensus decision-making on all major issues will take place prior to finalization. Where consensus decisions are not possible, such issues will be elevated to the next higher authority.
Informed (I)	Those who are kept up-to-date on progress, and with whom there is only an expectation of one-way communication.

a workflow system was able to bind together independent processes and create virtual project management.

It is likely that other project management tools will also be found to be very beneficial to system management, and both risk assessment and risk management have already been discussed. Stakeholder analysis, communication plans, and similar tools are recommended.

10

The Overlap of Systems and Frameworks

At this point, we can readily see that organizations are easily defined as a group of systems, since systems at their highest level should merely be defining and preserving best known practices to accomplish a defined business purpose. In addition, we can see that systems mapping creates a best practice operational plan within each office and program, so the composite of mapping the organization ensures that best practices span the organization. The analysis of performance through the review of each organizational system map also ensures the optimal performance of the entire organization.

Through use of the system management standard, discussed in Chapter 8, and the process management standard, it is therefore possible for each organization to systematically catalog what it believes to be the key functions (or systems) within each executive office and each program office. It can then map and score each such system to develop a leading measure of its likelihood of achieving "superior performance" or its current quality. While this book has not greatly discussed the process management standard, it is clear that any key processes discovered in this overall organizational mapping should be evaluated for maturity and capability, and that this process index will add another important adjunct to the overall organizational scorecard.*

One last means of testing the applicability of a system mapping approach for an organization would be to review the goals and roles of leadership and management, as described in the management literature. While many

---

* The Process Management Standard is maintained and updated by the American Society for Quality, Government Division, and a copy is available online on its Web page: www.asq.org/gov. It is also one of three standards presented by the author in his book *Quality Standards for Highly Effective Government*.

such lists of these goals and roles exist, the following is offered as a brief but thorough summary:

- Negotiate and define mission, purpose, and goals
- Build necessary processes and their capability
- Build necessary systems and their capability
- Prioritize tasks/resolve conflicts
- Assure task completion
- Provide accountability for resources
- Enable people through words, feedback, and training
- Evaluate performance, gaps in performance, and opportunities to improve

While most of these goals and roles are best performed by the chief executive officer and/or subordinate managers, the successful completion of all of them, and the evaluation of the operation of all of them, should be discussed by all and communicated to all—which is a definition of governance.

Defining a structure and pattern in which organizational resources can produce the intended result is generally considered the primary role of leadership, and its secondary goal is ensuring that the organization continues to produce a reliable and excellent result. These objectives require the practice of *oversight* through the use of quality assurance and quality control, risk assessment, risk management, and continuing process improvement. If we were to generalize, we could call this a *system of oversight*, as long as it was understood that it also includes quality assurance, quality management, and risk management. This system of oversight applies not only to product and service quality but also to the quality of the management structure itself.

Given that work does not always flow in pre-determined patterns and that planned resources are not always sufficient for all contingencies, it is also often thought that organizational governance should include a *system of decision-making* and a *system of resource allocation*. The system of decision-making needs to identify how the organization recognizes and analyzes issues for action and how these are then moved to evaluation and decision. These decisions may be focused in two specific areas: they may be decisions that reflect exceptions from the established pattern of organizational rules and processes, or they may reflect gaps in performance and opportunities to improve.

The system of resource allocation will typically evaluate the sufficiency of existing resources versus goals and will allocate scarce resources toward primary areas of risk, deficiency, or opportunity. Systems of resource allocation may also assist in the formulation and approval of new organizational projects.

Overall, the noted and defined systems provide a full, valid, and simple system structure for organizational leadership, and include

- Governance
- Oversight
- Decision-making
- Resource allocation

And to this list we should also add "organizational alignment," which is the last topic discussed in this chapter.

Hopefully, it would now not be beyond the skills of any reader of this book to take any one of these leadership systems and to perform the following steps:

1. Identify and name the system from which you are seeking optimized outputs
2. Identify its outputs and business purpose (or "aim")
3. Identify the principal activity groups associated with its intended value creation
4. Identify the output criteria of each principal activity group
5. Identify the influencing factors that are causes of successful outputs
6. Describe the attributes of successful performance of each principal activity group
7. Describe the indicators and measures of success for the activity groups
8. Describe the indicators and measures of failure for the activity groups
9. Identify the most feasible points of control for your system (the best achievable practice and a system operational plan)
10. Identify intervening variables within your system
11. Develop a risk management plan and risk management scenarios
12. Apply the system management standard to understand your system capacity and system maturity and the next steps for systems control and improvement efforts

Given that this is true, we have reached a new system of ordering entire organizations and a framework for the practice of excellence that has greater utility than those provided by the Criteria for Performance Excellence of the Malcolm Baldrige National Quality Award or the ISO 9001 Quality Management Standards of the International Organization for Standardization. While both have a place in the practice of organizational management, organizations will discover that a simple system management standard can revolutionize their practice and build in a much-needed agility and flexibility of application, which is difficult to do with ISO.

The practice of system management standards also creates a component of "severability" in organizational excellence, such that if one part of the organization loses interest in the foundations of excellence, the others also lose the incentive to continue. This has been the prevailing problem in the traditional practice of quality: that the primary motivating force for its continuation has of necessity come from the executive office, and it has been rewarded and continued only because of executive recognition—something the author refers to as "spotlight quality." The building up of the measurable practice of quality within the span of control of every supervisor and manager will build a "survivable" base of practice that will (hopefully) be impossible to extinguish. Most importantly, though, if the day arrives when both government and corporate auditors see value in the maintenance of system and process management standards, there will be an undeniable and continuing motivation to persist in their use.

ALIGNMENT OF SYSTEMS

The only missing piece in the organization-wide use of the system structure is the alignment of systems, which also presents the possibility of the application of the principles of Lean to systems. Now, we begin to see the fabric of an entire organizational mapping process: possible inter-connections that will often exist between systems (see Figure 10.1).

In this example, we can see numerous interdependencies, with the significant possibility of duplication and delay. So where the hard-to-get attention of specific subject matter experts is required for system success ("resources" in Figure 10.1), some systems may be starved for required

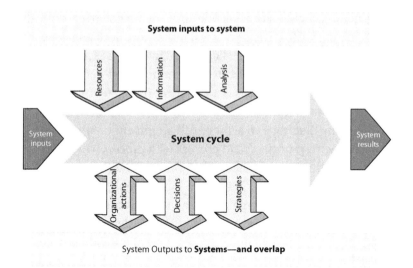

FIGURE 10.1
System inputs to system.

inputs regardless of their level of priority. Or if multiple systems required an input of "analysis," they could each be required to perform the same analysis ("duplication"), whereas by working together, they might perform better analysis and save resources.

This latter example was recently reinforced by the Lean quality manager in a large organization known to the author, who stated that the same analysis of areas of program performance and vulnerability was being performed by four separate offices in their organization: one by the Lean Quality Office in identifying future Lean projects, one by the risk management office, one through the development of the annual audit plan, and one by the strategic planning office! These offices were all competing for the precious time of senior executives to do similar interviews, surveys, analysis meetings, and document reviews. While we normally do not have a forum for evaluating the sources and causes of duplication, waste, and delay in executive functions, the comprehensive review of organizational system maps will lay the groundwork to do just that. This conclusion implies that organizations may want to establish a system of system alignment as part of their organizational plan.

The review and alignment of organizational systems is also a natural place to identify interdependencies between programs, which again, should be able to better perform the shared functions and get a better result with less resource use. In one recent example encountered by the author, a government agency field inspection unit was not sharing critical incident information with a license renewal unit whose licensing depended on the good standing of those same licensees. One kept a record of "bad performance," while the other tried to determine "good performance." The resolution of interdependencies is another means of streamlining, consistent with Lean practice.

Organizations that hope to achieve full alignment of systems with systems, systems with processes, and process with process will need to establish an organization-wide "system of alignment," but that system also will be easily designed using the guidelines in this book. Such an office will have the double benefit of being able to apply an annual Define, Measure, Analyze, Improve, and Control review to all systems and processes, to drive the continuing annual update and review of individual system maps with matching performance metrics, and to supercharge any existing Lean process efforts.

11

Wicked Problems, Logos, and the Future of System Science

In a very real sense, system management is the science of everything, and it provides a method for structuring, analyzing, and improving the results of any system—from the reduction of greenhouse gases to strategic planning. Its primary first ingredient is logos, a conscious will that wishes to influence the necessary parts of the natural world to accomplish a result. This is leadership in a very real sense, and system management is its blueprint. It is no coincidence that the title of this book includes the word "leadership," since the will to design any system, or all systems, will be a function of the desire of you, the reader, or of groups working together. This focused leadership, or logos, will provide both a leadership focus and a knowledge base to positively influence the future in whatever direction you choose to take it.

This book was obviously written to help structure human systems, generally within single organizations. But that does not mean that system management will not work in a much broader horizon, or that surprising new tools and applications cannot be derived from its use.

The concept of wicked problems was introduced in the late 1960s to describe problems that are difficult or impossible to solve because of incomplete and contradictory information sources, changing requirements, and interdependent causes. The question is: How can you create a different result when there are multiple and changing root causes that combine differently to create intervening events and also combine differently to create varying end results? The only way of course, is to look to system performance. The mechanistic approach of breaking things into progressively smaller parts will only waste time and create frustration, while the system approach will develop knowledge of generalized rules, best practices, stepping stones, drivers, and inhibitors—it is the future of human systems management.

A professional colleague was recently describing the problems he has encountered in corporate data mining and data management. His corporation has accumulated an impressive amount of data in many areas, and intermediate management is being confounded by various proposed uses and segmented presentations. Everyone knows there is gold in there, and all are spending a lot of time trying to find it. The professional literature on this subject is again raising vague terms of practice, including "feature selection" and "data wrangling," and is broadly debating how to proceed. They are looking at data mining as if it were a crystal ball that, if they look long enough and hard enough at, will tell them exactly what they need to do! What they are forgetting, however, is their need to lead.

The leadership perspective of system management suggests that the presentation of significant business questions in the form of a business purpose or aim and subsequent system mapping would assist in evaluating the value or structuring the presentation of data to achieve the best possible result. It might also identify the human and organizational components of its testing, distribution, and use.

Such a system approach could well describe an approach and deployment for the productive use of this data. It could also provide for the alignment of the data system within its host organization, reaching upward to the overall business purpose and reaching downward to the individual processes that are supported or controlled by that system. The efforts to align would create organizational synergy and open the door to eliminating barriers and encouraging synergistic relationships instead of suspicion or hostility.

Another colleague has been expressing frustration with the current and growing practice of developing and requiring new and additional processes for identifying and managing risk and the matching desire to expand audit functions to respond to risk. In her article "Evaluating Process Effectiveness to Reduce Risk," Christena Shepherd* states that where auditors do not have subject matter expertise in the area being audited, they cannot "adequately evaluate whether a process is effective and whether risk-based thinking has been included in process development."

---

* See "Evaluating Process Effectiveness to Reduce Risk," by Christena Shepherd, MAOM, ASQ-CMQ/QR, CQA. Jacobs/ ESSSA Group, NASA Marshall Space Flight Center. http://asq.org/gov/2017/08/process-management/a-framework-for-government-agency-quality-management-systems.pdf.

This results in a burden of non-value added work responding to speculative and prescriptive audit findings that are not "substantiated by the reported findings and conclusions" or that do not flow logically from the findings and conclusions" ... and are not "directed at resolving the cause of the identified deficiencies and findings."*

She notes, though, that where an organization is using a performance standard that defines its systems and processes and analyzes them for effectiveness, "it serves to preclude much of the subjectivity that might otherwise be injected into audit results." Shepherd adds that "[t]he relationship between risk-based thinking and effective processes (and systems) is simple and direct" and that a regularly updated management structure "incorporates risk-based thinking into the systems and processes as a matter of normal activity."

It is likely that there are many possible new benefits of system management, all of which will bring an objective and scientific method first to leadership. Then, through alignment, these benefits can be realized throughout the organization. System management presents a missing puzzle piece that is likely to unlock untold new benefits in the future.

---

* U.S. Government Auditing Standard (2011 Revision) Section 7.28, on appropriate audit recommendations.

Conclusion

There are many benefits in a system management approach that is structured to meet the needs of the future. Structured system management provides an agile and flexible framework for overall organizational improvement and a force for the long-term sustainability of its close, but organizationally incomplete, cousin—Lean process improvement. The inclusion of a uniform and empirical method for measuring the maturity of systems, as presented in this work, provides the next major platform for the deployment of quality science in our greater world and invites those in the quality profession to review, use, and suggest improvement to the new practice of systems science.

Appendix I: Lexicon of Key Terms

Achievable best practice	An agreed-on plan for the operation of a process or system that includes achievable tasks, actions, and performance levels. It is an adaptation of best known practice, reflecting available resources and priorities within a business environment
Best practice	A theoretical and future state reflecting the highest level of efficiency and effectiveness in product and service delivery
Best known practice	The documented operational practices that describe the methods that you and your knowledgeable colleagues believe are the very best you could achieve
Business purpose	The business value or purpose of a unit, program, or function. A description of its value or reason for existence. This term is used interchangeably with "mission."
Capability	The sustained, reliable production of process or system design requirements. The sustained production of error-free and value-added work without unnecessary wait time
Continuous improvement	The cyclical and routine use of performance evaluation and root cause analysis to identify and implement better system and process methods in pursuit of performance excellence
Effectiveness	A positive high level of achievement in meeting process design requirements and quality objectives
Efficiency	A positive low level of resource use in the operation of a process or system
Generic group practices	Generic group practices are not associated with a particular desired outcome or output and are believed to be associated with either a positive work environment or worker commitment to generalized goals
Indicators	Data or information that shows whether a goal or planned performance level was achieved. Indicators are checklist items or measures that are expected to be 100% complete. They are often leading or predictive measures that are fundamental to achieving process or system outputs
Influencing factors	Tasks or activity groups that are believed to be critical to achieving principal activity groups. The causes of success in achieving principal activity groups. The component parts of the system operational plan

(Continued)

(CONTINUED)

Key process/key system	Key processes and systems represent the primary responsibilities or assignments of individual managers or entire organizations. They are the processes and systems that create the primary value add of that group or organization or its most significant value areas
Lean	A management practice that is focused on the creation of error-free and waste-free work with only value-added task time and continuous flow
Maturity	Used in the context of the maturity of processes or systems, maturity refers to the existence of defined and proved methods for operations and a management structure to ensure the consistent and reliable delivery of optimal results through those processes and systems. It is sometimes also referred to as a deployment (a plan) and an approach (the assured execution of that plan) to ensure the delivery of optimal quality in products and services
Measures	Numeric values and other objective and quantitative indicators that provide feedback on performance levels. Generally a more generic expression than metrics
Metrics	Numeric values that express performance levels comparatively and relative to a scale of possible performance. Their relative ranking expresses average, good, and bad performance. They are objective and quantitative
Mission	The primary reason for existence of a business unit, program, or function. An expression of what it is intended to do. The value it seeks to create
Objective	The described goal of work activity. A goal expressed in terms of the desired result
Objective performance	An expression of performance level based on quantitative information, data, and verifiable first-person reports
Optimal performance	The consistent and reliable delivery of process or system design requirements and achievement of the highest level of success
Outcome	The secondary and larger-world impacts of the products and services created by a system or process. "Public safety" is an outcome of "community policing." Often related to an objective
Output	Specific tangible products and services created by a system or process, expressed in such a form that metrics can be used to determine the level or value of the output
Performance excellence	A preferred term for quality. Referring to the optimal performance possible from any process or system and focused on consistently and reliably meeting design (customer and stakeholder) requirements
Points of control	Points of control are defined points of time or events in an expected workflow that should trigger a manager's review, authorization, or approval and that use defined requirements as a review criterion. Defined points of control support a formal management review, appropriate controls, and a plan of quality assurance

(Continued)

(CONTINUED)

Principal activity groups	Coherent groups of activities that must be achieved in an order to obtain a defined outcome. These coherent groups may include: (1) actions; (2) products of thought and information; (3) defined products and services
Process design requirements	The defined requirements statement for any process or system. For a process, these requirements should focus on the measurable aspects of its output, while for systems, they will focus primarily on outcomes and only secondarily on outputs. This term augments "customer" requirements in that the customer represents only the next user of the product and service, while stakeholder requirements, along with regulatory and legal requirements, can be of equal or greater importance in a determination of acceptability of output
Process science	The use of process management tools to capably meet process design requirements. The continuous use of measurement and evaluation of process performance to create continuous improvement and quality
Productive components or work centers	Formal or informal groups of workers who are tasked with the management of a process, project, or system
Quality	Describes products and services that consistently and reliably meet defined requirements and that fulfill the needs of both immediate next users (customers) of those products and services and stakeholders (second-level users and those who have an interest in successful product and service delivery)
Quality management	Management practice focused on excellence in the delivered product
Quality science	The use of process management tools, combined with measurement and evaluation, to create continuous improvement and quality. Quality science also emphasizes an engaged and empowered workforce as a necessary foundation for achieving performance excellence
System management	Management practice that reflects the need to define key systems and structure achievable best practices for those systems, aligned with performance measures
Systems	Repetitive, cyclical, and output-specific structured work activities or functions
Systems science	The use of system management tools to capably meet systems design requirements. The continuous use of measurement and evaluation of system performance to create continuous improvement and quality

Appendix II: Auditable Quality Standards: Purpose and Origin

This book presents process management as a derivative of system management, with both supported by measurable and empirical practice standards—"auditable quality standards." Both are now new professional standards, adopted by the Government Division of the American Society for Quality, and both are referenced in this workbook.* Taken together, they provide the ability to clearly measure the quality potential (called *maturity*) of systems and processes. This objective ranking methodology also creates the basis of a scorecard of quality practice. The mandatory and continuing use of the process and system maturity standards in an organization will also make the innate management strength (or capacity) of each work group transparent. They will provide the first ever leading measure of quality practice in organizations. Through their use, the "goodness" or "badness" of each work unit is revealed, so that the practice of quality management (or its absence) will be apparent to everyone.

This system/process framework provides a leading measure of quality[†] and solves its biggest historical problem, which is sustainability. Where the use of quality practice is only evident in its results, managers can abandon the sustained use of quality science and mimic its positive results through short-term artifice. Through this chameleon effect and short-term operational strategies, many organizations can blindly forfeit a focus on quality practice without ever realizing the loss. This is particularly true in government, where a direct economic reward for excellence of operations does not exist. This shows the truth of the well-known saying: "If you cannot measure it, you cannot manage it."

Not only is the concept of structured system management practice new, but so is its measurement of the maturity of quality practice. This is provided through Auditable (or measurable) Quality Standards for

---

* Available through the ASQ Government Division Web page: http://asq.org/gov/quality-information/library/.
† See "Measuring Maturity, Quality Progress," September 2016. http://asq.org/quality-progress/2016/09/process-capability/measuring-maturity.html.

government, which have been adopted as an international standard for government by the American Society for Quality, Government Division. Even though these standards were first created for government, their application for the profit sector will have similar benefits.

There are three standards—the process management standard, the system management standard, and the aligned leadership objectives standard—all of which build on each other and progressively define an agile and dynamic quality structure. While the theory and structure are explained in the book *Auditable Quality Standards for Highly Effective Government*,* this book attempts to provide a how-to guide on the use and application of system management alone—which is an entirely new discipline in the practice of management.

In this way, system management should redefine the practice for the profession of management in the future and hold them accountable for these practices through the use of structured systems management *and* process management.

These standards look at the application of quality in a distinctly different way from the Baldrige Excellence Framework or the ISO 9001 management standards, in that they can be developed from the front line service level upward, or from the top-down, or in a collaborative interchange between the two. There is also an easy severability of quality components in an organization, so that a single program office or process manager can implement them alone just as easily as all components of an organization can easily align ALL the process management efforts they have standardized in each product or service delivery office independently.

The standards allow each productive component of an organization to separately self-identify, self-organize as a process or system, and separately adapt and improve. This severable quality structure ensures the survivability of the quality function during periods of changing top leadership and rapid recovery when and if leadership again becomes committed to quality practices. It also allows agile adaptation to changing conditions without any restraint or excessive requirement for a leadership-driven framework of any type. Clearly, there are many benefits from the use of the standards.

---

* Mallory, Richard, 2018. *Quality Standards for Highly Effective Government*. Second Edition, Taylor & Francis.

In short, systems management discards traditional mainstream thinking about developing high-performing organizations and can re-invent quality practice everywhere. This workbook has been created as an easy-to-use guide on these new standards and how they can be used to enable powerful new leadership results everywhere.

Appendix III: Systems Management as an Agile Quality Framework

(This appendix is a white paper on system management that was published by the American Society for Quality Government Division. While much of its content is also presented in the book, it is offered here because it includes some additional thinking that may be helpful to those initiating system management efforts.).

An essential but broadly overlooked management practice for Government Executives and Program Managers is to identify and manage their critical (or "key") management systems.* Only through such systems management is it possible to understand and document the most positive practices, consistently replicate positive organizational results, and to learn and improve based on past practice. This management discipline will also allow executives the ability to learn and improve on their current achievement and to better respond to changing conditions[†].

The practice of key systems management has recently been identified by the American Society for Quality (ASQ) Government Division as the next frontier of quality management, and one that should change the fundamental expectations of all public sector managers. The failure to manage predictable and cyclical key systems is a failure to marshal the greatest organizational wisdom and to support organizational excellence to the

---

* Systems can be defined as a network of interdependent components that work together to accomplish a purpose. This is the definition of system provided by W. Edwards Deming in *The New Economics*, 1993. Massachusetts Institute of Technology, Center for Advanced Engineering, pp. 94–118.

[†] The author demonstrates that the highest level leadership systems, including governance itself, can be brought under the analytic methods of continuous quality improvement through application of systems management. This management framework, along with a process management standard and an aligned leadership objectives standard, are outlined in his book *Quality Standards for Highly Effective Government*, Trafford Publications, 2014.

greatest extent possible. It is also a failure in the adaptation and use of the known beneficial practices of Lean and Quality Science.*

Where systems are thought about as functions of control, authorization, decision-making, or oversight, they are often viewed as either isolated activities or sequential decisions that are only manageable through spontaneous or consultative decision-making by individual managers. This kind of thinking leads to the conclusion that the actions of executives are somehow above or isolated from the application of Lean and Quality Science. This in turn leads these managers to believe that the actions, events, and activities they use for decision-making and program direction should not and cannot be standardized and documented. They incorrectly believe that executive actions should be created by their individual intuition and contemporaneous judgments, which also means that they are reactive and insulated from organizational wisdom! This belief must change.

In fact, *all* systems have repetitive and predictable components that are ideally suited to fact-based management, and the principles of quality science. This article therefore presents the perspective that approach and deployment of such systems is fundamental to excellence in management, with the development of mature managed key systems as an auditable and documentable goal. A focus on mature managed systems will standardize patterns of practice with the greatest history of positive results, build in risk management and scenario analysis, and support dependent processes throughout the organization—which in fact are the suppliers or customers of management systems!

IDENTIFICATION OF KEY SYSTEMS

The best way of beginning on the path of "finding" and defining such systems and adequately describing them is to develop an extended "mission" statement for each executive and program office, which can also be described as its business purpose. Managers of the office may then be able to see systems that correspond to each subcategory of the named business

---

* Quality Science is defined as the tools and knowledge associated with quality management. It had its origins in the Toyota Production System of the 1970s and embraces a broad body of professional knowledge focused on doing work right the first time. It is used as the basis of the U.S. Baldrige Performance Excellence Program and the Japanese Deming Award. It is embodied in the Body of Knowledge maintained by the American Society for Quality.

purpose, or they can proceed onto further analysis by listing the primary objectives of their position or office. Once such headings of "purpose" are established, they can be further tested by the defined outputs and outcomes intended to be delivered through each "purpose" or "system." Those who have used the SIPOC* tool may see a close parallel, and will find that systems are defined through identification of inputs and intended outputs.

While each executive's list of roles, and thus of "systems," may be long, they should only focus on the primary areas of value creation—which we will call "key systems." This is due to the fact that key systems management is a tool used for improvement of performance, and improvement activity requires management time; therefore, only key systems should be prioritized. This will require the selection of one or a few such key systems from a longer list. This list should describe what the office is established to do, and should have a clear link to organizational mission, purpose or functionality.

INITIAL EVALUATION OF EACH KEY SYSTEM

In this step the manager must perform an initial evaluation of the current performance of each defined system, and juxtapose that with its current results. This provides feedback on its current, or baseline, performance and a first effort to define its desired performance. A list of system design requirements (similar to customer requirements) can be established in this way. This may be done both through identification of who uses the products of the system, and by defining the attributes of the outputs and outcomes that are desired.

This line of inquiry and documentation will also reveal which organizational systems or processes may provide inputs into the defined system (and are therefore its suppliers) and which are users of system outputs (and are therefore its customers). The use of the principles of the "voice of the customer" then follows, and provides an excellent way to validate and quantify the system output requirements. This in turn will enhance the assessment of its current performance, and will *identify areas of improvement*.

---

* An analytic method that defines Supplier, Input, Process, Output, and Customer. In this case, we would substitute the "Key System" name for the word "Process".

It is also recognized that systems may have associated characteristics imposed by law, regulation, standards, or policy that also must be included. So, a decision about hiring, for example, may have additional necessary characteristics. Perhaps it will need supporting analysis, a cost-benefit ratio, a risk analysis, an action request and a communication plan. It may even need a decision in light of competing professional opinions about need or benefit.* These can be regarded as corollary outputs, and built into the overall system requirement. Since this overall requirement is clearly more than a traditional end-user customer requirement, we have developed the term "design requirement" to reflect the fact that many of its attributes are imposed by other authority.

All the system design requirements taken together with its defined performance metrics and indicators provide the characteristics of what we will call the object of value creation or "OVC." This new term is provided to reflect the fact that systems—like projects—may have variance in what is to be included from cycle to cycle.† The OVC can be expected to need updates from cycle to cycle, which emphasizes the need to identify and manage the "intervening variables" that cause that variation. Scenario analysis then becomes a new tool of systems management to reflect that variation.

DEFINITION OF THE SYSTEM

Systems have a triple constraint. In the first instance, the requirement of the OVC in each system cycle cannot be known in advance. It may vary, and this variance includes both the basic nature of the thing or things being worked on (the input), and the characteristics of the work that is required that leads to the end product (the desired output).‡ Secondly,

---

* Project Management is also a form of systems management, and this article provides a specific and uniform framework for that discipline as well. The definition of the output and outcome requirements for projects is particularly necessary, as is the balancing of the attributes of scope, schedule, budget, and quality.

† Processes tend to have more specific and quantifiable outputs, with fewer attributes, while systems have more attributes and those that require assignment of general and descriptive attributes, with some that require balancing of competing values (i.e., "highest ethical standards").

‡ A classic example might be the system of strategic planning, where both the preparation and research inputs may vary greatly from cycle to cycle, as may the group of experts asked to participate.

and in direct parallel with project management, the resource group and the commitment of resources to any systems cycle is variable. Third, the required path (or map) of the work output may necessarily vary. These variables all require attention and calibration of the system map at the start of each cycle.

The mapping of a system will then first require a calibration of each cycle, followed by an update of its "map." This mapping activity must consider three design categories including a baseline system definition that defines those system activities that are known and constant, those that vary but are within the normal span of control of the organization, and those that vary and are outside its span of control.

Process mapping then provides a rudimentary model for systems management, and especially for those system activities that are known and constant. These should be documented in what is called, "Principal Activity Groups," illustrated in Figure AIII.1.

Systems mapping must show the principal activities, actions, and check-gates that are required, including the inputs and steps for the system's output. The inputs and steps in the diagram can be considered "influencing factors" and are included to the extent that they are known to contribute to or influence the achievement of the defined "activity group" or milestone.

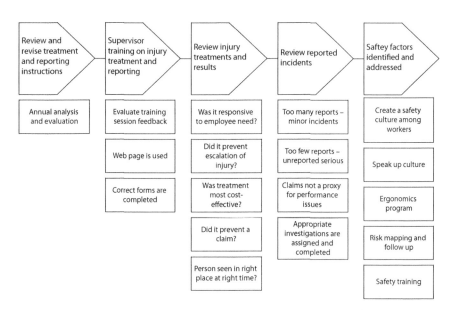

FIGURE AIII.1
System of safety oversight and injury prevention.

Here the use of the project management system is directly analogous, with its defined key activity groups of initiation, planning, execution, control, and closing.* The idea of project "check-gates" from project management principles is also appropriate, because it suggests a series of review points through which the OVC must pass.

In *system management*, we should then define a map of such activities, actions, and check-gates that are subordinate parts of contributors to the necessary output.

As noted, each check-gate, or Principal Activity Group, is known to be a contributor to the output requirement of "Safety Factors Identified and Addressed," and this "map" reflects the known repetitive factors of the positive result. In addition, the subordinate contributing factors have also been identified.

Once established, an effort must be made to ensure that system's actions and flow are predictable and reliable. The control factors most relevant to systems management are:

1. Resource availability
2. Defined output and outcomes, and their influencing factors
3. Response to common intervening variables (perhaps through scenario analysis)
4. Risk management (for response to factors beyond the span of control)

Resource availability is perhaps most commonly seen and discussed with regard to project management. Often it requires that assigned personnel and resources are available, accountable to the system requirements (or project), and focused on its goal. In another similarity, the use of a RACI matrix[†] to define Responsible, Accountable, Consulted, and Informed personnel at each task and activity, is a major system improvement. This kind of resource group control must be the result of leadership and communication. For this reason, the resource groups and accountability at each action step or milestone should be defined.

In the use of systems mapping for predictable cycles of output or for projects, the chronological tracking of check-gate completion would be

---

* Project Management Institute, Project Management Body of Knowledge.
[†] From the Project Management Body of Knowledge: The definition of roles for each major activity group include Responsible, Accountable, Consulted, Informed (RACI).

paramount, along with checking for completion of output requirements at each check-gate.

Where common variables are involved, scenario analyses should be developed for each variant to reflect the best practice reaction. So, for projects, scenario analysis should include contract change requests and change management. Where known risks affect the system, a risk management plan should be in place.

Finally, in order to evaluate what is to be accomplished at each step (outputs) and to evaluate whether the subordinate contributing factors that are currently in place address an excellent outcome, then requirements for completion of each check-gate should be developed. In that sense, the systems map should look like the Figure AIII.2.

Overall, the systems map should define OVCs and responsive actions, and show where intervening risks must be managed. Contingency plans, communication plans, and communication protocols should also match scenario analysis. Variance in the assumptions and constraints imposed on actions and outputs should also be quantified as a part of the analysis of predictable variation within the system. Note that each Activity/ Action Group can be seen to influence or contribute to completion of the defined Milestone and Check-Gate.

Definition of the system should provide the best known plan for achieving the purposes for which it was commissioned (its system requirements), and should describe an approach and deployment for the operation. It should also provide for the alignment of the system within its host organization, reaching upward to the overall business purpose, and reaching downward to the individual processes that are supported or controlled by

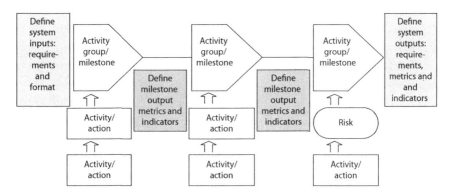

FIGURE AIII.2
Methods of systems management.

that system. The efforts to align all systems creates organizational synergy, and opens the door to eliminate barriers and to encourage synergistic relationships everywhere.

Finally, once the system is defined in this manner, and a formalized feedback loop is in place, it allows systems managers to identify points of constraint and waste, and to apply the tools of Lean and Continuous Improvement. In this way, structured systems management provides an agile and flexible framework for overall organizational improvement, and a force for the long-term sustainability of its close cousin, Lean Process Improvement.

The author believes that the definition of a uniform and empirical method of measuring the maturity of systems will be the next major platform for the deployment of Quality Science in our greater world, and invites those in the quality profession to review, use, and suggest improvement to the following Systems Management Standard.*

The System Management Standard, complete version, is available at www.asq.org/gov/ within its quality information section.

---

* The System Management Standard is provided as Featured Content on the ASQ Government Division Web page at: http://asq.org/gov/. Additional support materials are available in the "Library" section at that Web address. The use of system management within a comprehensive change model for government is presented in the book *Quality Standards for Highly Effective Government*, available from ASQ at: https://asq.org/quality-press/display-item?item=P1591.

Appendix IV: Systems Management to Launch the Next Era of Quality

(Similarly to Appendix III, this appendix is also a white paper on systems science, published by the American Society for Quality Government Division. It is provided here to introduce the reader to General Systems Theory, and the intellectual framework of Structured System Management).

Almost 50 years ago Dr. W. Edwards Deming announced that systems management was fundamental to what we can now call quality science,* and he introduced a "system of profound knowledge"[†] as a framework for transformation of our organizational work and our entire economy.[‡] He said that "An integral part of the system of profound knowledge is appreciation for a system." But while his system of profound knowledge got a lot of discussion at the time, most of its contemporary application has been limited to the "profound knowledge of variation," and to process standardization and process improvement. The most recent frameworks for both are currently described as Lean Six Sigma, Kaizen or 5S, and all represent what can be called forms of process science.

However, there is a matched partner to process science in systems science—the documentation and improvement of systems. The quality profession has failed to provide further exploration of systems as free-standing entities, in the same manner that it has for processes. The professional advancement of systems thinking has been almost entirely relegated to their use as control mechanisms for the comprehensive and top-down leadership frameworks of ISO and Baldrige, and efforts to explore systems

---

* A term adopted by the ASQ Government Division with this definition: "The tools and knowledge associated with quality management with its origins in the Toyota Production System of the 1970s, and embracing a broad body of professional knowledge focused on doing work right the first time. Used as the basis of the U.S. Baldrige Performance Excellence Program and the Japanese Deming Award. Embodied in the Body of Knowledge maintained by the American Society for Quality."

[†] Deming, W. E., 1993. *The New Economics.* Massachusetts Institute of Technology, Center for Advanced Engineering, pp. 94–118.

[‡] Deming, W. E., 1986. *Out of the Crisis.* Cambridge, MA: MIT, Center for Advanced Educational Services.

as free-standing entities that exist outside of these comprehensive organizational models has been lost. It is the author's position that this is the single biggest oversight of modern quality practice. Also, that a quantum leap in quality practice is now possible by a renewed focus on the identification and improvement of free-standing systems outside of comprehensive organizational focus, with the same independent rigor of professional practice that has been given to process standardization and continuous process improvement.

This renewed focus on systems can be called the development of "systems science," and this article will describe systems, systems science, and the importance of a systems management standard. It will provide a critique of the perceived shortcomings of Baldrige* and ISO† in creating a dynamic and agile means of achieving the full benefits of systems management.

This discussion must start with a definition of what a system is, and how it differs from a process. Dr. Deming himself defined a system as "a network of interdependent components that work together to try to accomplish the aim of the system." Taking a holistic view of what can be found in his works, we might speculate that he believed that a human system was a group of human and other resources (machines, methods, materials and the like) that has some ability to be controlled by leadership toward a valuable purpose that can be defined as an "aim."

We can see that a system itself is a thing from which we are trying to obtain a consistent and reliable output and outcome—and specifically, from which we are trying to eliminate variation. So we can postulate that the goal of quality science and that of systems management is the same: Our intent is to manage and improve our processes and systems to achieve a reliable and predictable result. So what is the difference between systems and processes? Are they two words that have almost the same or identical meaning?

Actually Dr. Deming himself gives us an important clue toward the differences, in his reference to a "network of interdependent components." The author does not know for certain, but it seems reasonable to assume that Dr. Deming was influenced by General Systems Theory. General

---

* Criteria for Performance Excellence of the Malcolm Baldrige National Quality Award, jointly maintained by the Department of Commerce National Institute for Standards and Technology and the American Society for Quality.
† International Organizational for Standardization (ISO), and its 9000 Series standards for Quality Management in Organizations.

Systems Theory is perhaps the oldest science, and it describes the efforts of early humans to decipher the operations of natural systems such as weather, seasons, ocean currents, and the behavior of plants and animals. It is observed that early humans observed and learned about these broad patterns, and initiated structured human strategies—early human systems—to make natural systems work better for the productive good of the group.

Every deliberate effort of early human tribes, and the latter day efforts of most structured human business enterprise are such systems or subsystems—attempting to derive value by creating human organizations that can positively influence complex external forces. So we can see that early forms of productive enterprise like agriculture, animal herding, pottery making, and the creation of ships, were alternately created by the broad application of "rules of knowledge" (achieved through the application of human systems) and by specific, controlled activity (process). In this scheme the sowing of seed for wheat or barley was a process, while growing and harvesting the crop was part of a human system. The building of a ship was often an early human process, while the navigation of ships was a body of knowledge, or a system! So perhaps the first necessary practice of systems management is to develop a series of strategies and actions—for example, regarding how to obtain and sow seed, cultivate a plowed field and harvest a crop. Only through development of knowledge with the strategies and actions to deploy that knowledge can we create a human system that will influence larger natural systems and provide a beneficial human result. Once developed, the results of such systems can be tested and improved to reduce their variation over time.

We can see that systems science must also provide knowledge and experience that allows for a broader range of possible actions to respond to the intervening factors ("common cause" variation) that comes from our larger natural systems. In other words the successful exploitation of agriculture had to respond to natural variation in factors like the supply of seed, early and later spring-time, flood and drought, insect infestations, labor shortages and similar challenges. These systems included much greater year-to-year variation that their simpler process counterparts, like plowing a field. So we see that systems science grapples with a more uncertain environment and more apparently uncontrollable intervening factors than does process science, and with a less certain knowledge of best practices defined by steps where "a" follows "b" and goes before "c." Looking to more modern general systems theory, we can see that this brand of science provided first steps for embracing "... the concept of order and man's general need for imaging (or establishing) his world as an orderly cosmos within an unordered chaos."* The concept of an orderly cosmos is to systems management what "error-free work" is to process management.

One key principle of systems science theories is confirmed by Dr. Deming's statement that a system is "a network of interdependent components that work together..." It is immediately apparent from the preceding discussion that early human systems and most modern business enterprise operate in an environment where it does not control all the essential components, and it must often be responsive to a variety of changing conditions rather than controlling a fixed environment. One of the distinguishing characteristics of systems management is that it must create a mixture of *value creating actions* that can be clearly defined and fixed, with *responsive actions* that evaluate and respond to changing conditions. A systems flowchart will be possible, but it will have to include both explicit action steps (like those in process maps) with categorical action steps (unique to systems maps). Both types of "steps" will need to seek to analyze and respond to intervening conditions to create a more reliable result.

Dr. Deming's statements also imply another of the differences in the notation that the system components "work together." This combined with the concept of components that are "interdependent" implies that human systems depend on leadership and on structure to influence the component parts to work together at all, and effectively. In addition, there is a need to link systems, with macro-systems linking to natural systems, and successive sub-systems defining the enterprise of men (organizations), linking down to its sub-systems and processes. We can then see that the principle of "alignment" has profound meaning, and that the linking of processes and systems reflects the rich network of activity that must exist in the highest performing organizations (Figure AIV.1).

Another key area of exploration comes from an understanding that there can be strong or weak systems in each organization's network. A strong system must benefit from leadership and commitment of its

---

* Skyttner, Lars, 2005. *General Systems Theory.* Hackensack, NJ: World Scientific Publishing, p. 51.

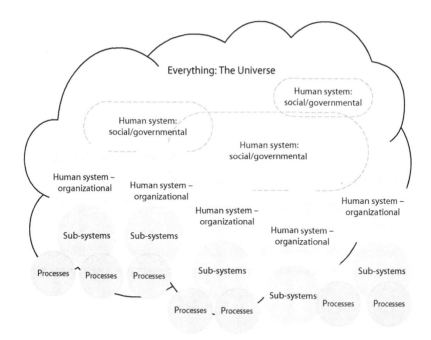

FIGURE AIV.1
Cloud represents all of human existence.

human resources, which is in part motivated by its purpose, and its ability to build its resource base to protect its continuation and survival. Indeed this is the difference between entrepreneurial organizations and volunteer organizations, or between formally commissioned organizational structures and informal organizational structure—the ability of leadership to reward, incentivize or discourage participation.

Lars Skyttner* states: "A system is distinguished from its parts by its organization. Thus a random assembly of elements constitutes only a structureless mass unable to accomplish anything ... To qualify for the name system, two conditions apart from organization have to be present: continuity of identity and goal directedness. Something that is not able to preserve its structure amid change is never recognized as a system ... Reduced to everyday language we can express it as any structure that exhibits order, pattern and purpose."[†]

---

* Skyttner, Lars, 2005. *General Systems Theory.* Hackensack, NJ: World Scientific Publishing.
[†] Ibid, p. 57.

These differences are more fully explained by the unifying theory of work management,* that is new to quality science, and that asserts that all work has some repetitive factors and common resources, and that managers have the ability to learn from past experience and constructively apply that learning to the future so that better results, or improvement, can take place.† The specific means of testing, standardizing and using this knowledge varies depending on the work structure available to implement it, however, and quality science is primarily focused on implementation of explicit forms of value creation that are deployed through processes and systems.‡

It is the factors of a common, known environment, and shared and established resources that allow managers to standardize best practices for creation of standard outputs, and the existence of "common-" and "standard-cause" factors in working environments that create variation in outputs (Figure 2.2).

Given that projects, systems, and processes are the only means we have of creating work in an organization, we can easily understand that all have some level of specificity of steps and methods, and some level of control of their environment and resource group. So ALL THREE are subject to the standardization of best practices—the subject of Quality Science. And upon reflection, we can see that projects themselves are also a form of human system—only with a few specific characteristics. So projects and systems must be subject to the same kind of quality improvement—including methods and tools—that processes are, with the sole variation being the specificity of best practice steps that can be defined, the ability to control the environment and the productive apparatus, the ability to structure a focused group of workers and methods, and the uniformity of control that can be imposed by leadership. Indeed, there is now a fundamental and logical basis to the assertion that scientific systems management is the greatest missed opportunity in quality practice.

One of the most important recognition of systems that exists in modern quality science is the understanding that leadership is a system, and that

---

* Mallory, Richard, 2014. *Quality Standards for Highly Effective Government.* Trafford Publishing, pp. 14–15, 38–39.

† It is the author's belief that this is what Dr. Deming was referencing in his "theory of knowledge" as one part of the system of profound knowledge. Specifically that all process control and systems control is an expression of human learning and continuous improvement.

‡ Learning theory notes that knowledge can also be applied to work through cognitive and tacit actions of individuals that are shaped by experience and training.

quality management and process quality control are also systems. Indeed, most of the process science such as it now exists, is defined in both the ISO and the Baldrige standards, as described in the following:

ISO 9001 requires systems including:

- Establishment of customer requirements
- Control of production
- Verification
- Configuration management
- Risk management

Baldrige requires organization-wide systems for

- Leadership and management
- Strategy development and implementation
- Business systems (that incorporate customer requirements)
- Organizational learning
- Information and knowledge

The only problem that may exist with implementation of these larger framework systems are that they pre-suppose that these suggested and over-arching systems are necessary in all situations.* They impose an organizational review from the top-down that involves all managers in trying to create and align with these specific macro-systems. Given that we know that all efforts of this type take the time and attention of every-one in the organization, they could remove discretionary time from any other improvement efforts in favor of the creation and maintenance of these suggested systems. And while these suggested systems are believed to be essential in most organizations most times, where such frameworks are implemented they will replace a focus on a more localized and bottom-up approach that could be much more agile and important to the survival of the organization. The top-down effort will most certainly discourage a bottom-up systems management strategy.

---

* The author is aware that neither Baldrige nor ISO is prescriptive, and that organizations can tailor and scale their systems implementation of these frameworks. This does not, however, remove the criticism that these top-down efforts do not emphasize a localized systems management focus in each work unit, and that they may eliminate the discretionary time and leadership focus necessary to implement alternate systems management strategies.

Likewise, where such top-down frameworks are later abandoned by a change in top leadership, it is likely that none of the subordinate efforts will be incentivized to maintain a localized systems management effort. In short, there is a primary need and benefit to have localized systems management throughout an organization, whether or not it exists at the highest level. It only makes sense that such a scheme will be consistently and immediately supportive of quality practices that can adapt and change to a changing environment. It will be much more agile.

We can now see that there must be a vast number of systems that exist in organizations just as there are a vast number of processes, and that not all exist throughout the organization or capture senior leadership attention. Organizational management tells us that we depend on IT systems management, human resource systems, project management systems, budget systems, research and development systems and many others. Even knowledge management is a system, because each organization must have methods and means associated with learning, recording its knowledge, and making it available to those who need it. We can see that each of these systems exist in organizations now, formally and informally, and with varying degrees of order, pattern, and purpose. The challenge then of systems management is to get organizations to recognize the formal and informal systems on which they now depend, and which are key to their progress, and to increase their reliable and positive results (quality)!

The present-day reliance on only the suggested and defined systems of ISO and Baldrige forecloses an affirmative responsibility of all executives and managers to manage their unique local systems, and through upward alignment, to create an overall better support system for all organizational processes. The existing focus on any set of mandated macro-system implies that system management should be practiced only top-down, and certainly not bottom-up! There is no realization that some important systems management may be done only in localized business units and with no connection to higher systems in any way.

The idea of auditable quality standards* enters from this perspective: That process management and systems management should be an affirmative responsibility of all executives, managers, and supervisors, and the only pre-eminent role of senior managers should be in aligning the

---

* Mallory, Richard, 2018. *Auditable Quality Standards for Highly Effective Government.* Second Edition, Taylor & Francis. A summary is also available at: http://videos.asq.org/new-look-at-quality-systems-auditable-standards.

systems that lower levels define, and in filling gaps to more fully support front-line processes. This perspective is the only one that ensures that organizations are agile and able to dynamically respond to change, with or without senior executive leadership. Indeed, the "flat" or self-directed organizations of the future that have been lauded by books like Holocracy* depend on a leadership structure of some kind, and the practice of process management combined with free-standing systems management is the only quality framework that holds this potential.

Auditable quality standards build on this framework, and present the premise that process maturity standards, systems maturity standards, and the strength and achievability of the leadership structure (or "aligned systems objectives") are the primary and only forces that create the strength of all human systems.† Put bluntly, it is argued that process management, with systems management, are the most fundamental and basic elements of quality science. They open a window where quality implementation can arise and be deployed through the independent actions of many managers and supervisors. They can therefore drive the agility, reliability and predictability (or "quality") of all human systems.

These three standards are definable and measurable through auditable quality standards, as have recently been adopted by the ASQ Government Division,‡ and thus create the ability to completely re-invent quality practice. For the first time, there is the ability to access a uniform and empirical measure of quality in organizations, and the basis of an easy-to-use and uniform scorecard.

The systems management standard depends on measured evaluation of three measurable aspects of systems including:

1. Known, comprehensive, and logical systems management
2. Effective use and feedback
3. Evaluation and improvement

The first criteria regarding the known, comprehensive and logical systems is responsive to the ideas of order, pattern and purpose as noted by Skyttner. It argues that a structured and focused leadership structure

---

* Robertson, B. J., 2015. *Holocracy: The New Management System for a Rapidly Changing World.* Henry Holt and Company.
† Ibid, Mallory.
‡ They are available as "QSG Summary 9-15-15" on the Government Division Web page at: asq.org/ gov.

should exist, with a clear established purpose, and with some kind of a documented systems process flow that includes explicit action steps with categorical actions, and each of those with steps that will analyze and respond to intervening conditions. So for example, a State government may have an emergency response system that looks like Figure AIV.2.

The second criteria, regarding "effective use and feedback," suggests that some kind of systematic deployment takes place, and that structure exists to ensure that the standardized portions of the system operation can reliably be replicated. It also suggests that metrics are in place regarding system outputs and outcomes, and that there is evidence that the system creates its intended value.

The third criteria suggest that there is evidence of periodic review and improvement of both means and methods of system delivery, and that there is data to support its improvement cycles.

About 10 years ago the Baldrige Criteria for Performance Excellence were amended to include the concept of ADLI, which is itself a systems evaluation structure. ADLI stands for approach, deployment, learning, and improvement, and this gives systems science another toolset for evaluating whether systems in organizations have been standardized, whether requirements have been established, whether it has metrics to define its

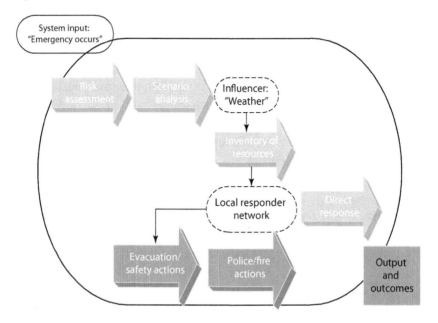

FIGURE AIV.2
Crisis response system.

success, and whether successive cycles of improvement ("learning") have taken place, and can be demonstrated.

These terms must sound very familiar to those involved in process science, and correctly implies that many of the tools of process science also can apply to systems. In other words, the efficiency and effectiveness of these systems can be controlled through standardization, and improved through continuous improvement! The scientific management of systems, with the same focus and attention as the scientific management of processes, has been the greatest missed opportunity in quality practice, and that a rededication to structured systems management has the potential to re-invent quality practice.

HIERARCHY OF SYSTEMS

The systems management standard is based on the concept of hierarchy of systems. This is the realization that all systems are defined within higher systems above, and sub-systems below, and that the concept of productive control begins with a definition of boundaries in which quality control can be exercised. So the leadership structure in human systems is an essential beginning point.

Christena Shepherd states that "accomplishment of the agency's mission in terms of its mission realization lifecycle," is the beginning point of organizational management, and that "this top level need or expectation must then be broken down ('decomposed') into its constituent parts and processes."* In effect then, we can see a hierarchy of systems within each organization, in which each executive manager has a role to identify, standardize (to the extent possible), and improve the systems they manage and that are essential to the value creation proposition of their span of control. This can be done either broadly and interpretively through a systems management framework, of empirically and uniformly through a systems management standard.

---

* Shepherd, Christena C., 2015. "A Framework for Government Agency Quality Management Systems." ASQ Government Division News, Winter.

MANAGEMENT OF SYSTEMS

So we can see that one important rule in our study of systems, is that systems must have a broader and less-well-defined specific outcomes—both overall and at each specific step. If we are looking at complex, high-level systems such as government, we can establish generalized outcomes of "justice," "equality" and "rules of law," but we see at the outset that it will be difficult to carefully define the "categorical action steps" and corresponding measures showing the relative achievement of each. It will be possible, however, to define the desired outcome of each, some known and applicable principles of knowledge (or "best practices"), and even to test the relative achievement of each to some extent through scientific testing. Perhaps we can do mapping of our government systems, but their "flow" will be a series of systems maps that show activities such as elections, creation of legislation, and judicial review of laws.

These same principles will hold true for the mapping of systems and sub-systems within organizations, in that alignment between the systems will be necessary, and that the highest level systems maps will need to align with lower level systems, and eventually with processes. As systems give way to sub-systems, the relative level of environmental control will be greater and reliable performance will be more predictable. And since the mapping of systems must be limited to higher-level activities, (i.e., "hold an election") rather than the more specific "tasks" of process science, then the primary tools of problem solving will be different. The author finds that the tools of root cause analysis, force field analysis, and inter-relationship diagraphs are more conducive to discovering the areas of improvement for systems "activities," and are the best tools for their improvement.

Overall it is believed that a focus by quality professionals on systems science and systems mapping has enormous potential to re-invent quality practice in the 21st century, especially when combined with the uniform and empirical tools provided by the process management standard and the systems management standard. These improvements taken together provide enormous potential for the improvement of all human enterprise.

Bibliography

Ackoff, R.L. and Emery, F.E. (2008). *On Purposeful Systems*. New Brunswick, NJ: Transaction Publishers.

Alter, S. (2006). *The Work System Method*. Larkspur, CA: Work System Press.

Brassard, M. and Ritter, D. (1994). *The Memory Jogger 2: Tools for Continuous Improvement and Effective Planning*. Methuen, MA: Goal/QPC.

Deming, W.E. (1986). *Out of the Crisis*. Cambridge, MA: MIT, Center for Advanced Educational Services.

Dixon, N.M. (2000). *Common Knowledge: How Companies Thrive by Sharing What They Know*. Boston, MA: Harvard Business School Press.

Ishikawa, K. (1985). *What Is Total Quality Control? The Japanese Way*. Englewood Cliffs, NJ: Prentice-Hall.

Kasse, T. (2008). *Practical Insight into CMMI*. Norwood, MA: Artech House.

Madison, D.J. (2005). *Process Mapping, Process Improvement and Process Management: A Practical Guide to Enhancing Work and Information Flow*. Chico, CA: Paton.

Mallory, R.E. (2014). *Quality Standards for Highly Effective Government*. Indianapolis, IN: Trafford Publishing.

Mintzberg, H. (1979). *The Structuring of Organizations*. Englewood Cliffs, NJ: Prentice-Hall.

National Institute of Standards and Technology, U.S. Department of Commerce (2017). *Baldrige Excellence Framework*. Gaithersburg, MD: National Institute of Standards and Technology, U.S. Department of Commerce.

Project Management Institute. (2013). *Project Management Body of Knowledge: PMBOK Guide*. Newtown Square, PA: PMI.

Senge, P.M. (1990). *The Fifth Discipline*. New York, NY: Doubleday/Random House.

Sharp, A. and McDermott, P. (2009). *Workflow Modeling*. Norwood, MA: Artech House.

Skyttner, L. (2005). *General Systems Theory*. Singapore: World Scientific Publishing.

Verardo, D. (2000). *Managing the Strategic Planning Process*. Alexandria, VA: American Society for Training and Development.

Wren, D.A. (1994). *The Evolution of Management Thought*. New York, NY: Wiley.

Afterword

I truly believe that system science can positively and forever transform the success of human organizations. Those who know me know that my singular career goal has been to find a way to make quality practice sustainable and universally practiced as a means of developing human excellence everywhere. I am excited about this book because it represents an important step toward the achievement of that goal.

The realization that systems can be managed on an individual basis will change leadership from a mythical and personality-based practice to one that is scientific and accountable for results. In coming to this realization, I must give credit to the U.S. National Quality Award and its Framework for Performance Excellence, which developed its Approach, Deployment, Learning, and Integration (ADLI) model perhaps ten years ago and challenged everyone who managed systems to develop a system approach and deployment that were capable of learning and innovation. Despite having the complete conceptual framework, however, they offered none of the specifics provided in this book.

There have been many colleagues and friends who have offered their continuing support and encouragement in this work, and I am especially thankful to the Leadership Council of the American Society for Quality Government Division overall, including Mark Abrams, Marc Berson, John Baranzelli, Brian DeNiese, Christena Shepherd, Mary Jo Caldwell, Josh Smith, Bonnie Gaughan-Bailey, Janice Stout, and Mendy Richard. Among those, I would like to offer special thanks to Christena Shepherd of the NASA Marshall Space Flight Center, who has read and commented on every system management white paper and every version of this book. I am also particularly thankful to my friend Denzil Verardo, a member of the California State Senate Cost Control Commission, who has also read every version of this book.

Lastly, I would like to offer recognition to my wife, Cathy, who has encouraged me at every step of this journey.

Index